MASTER THE MEDIA

TO ATTRACT
YOUR
IDEAL CLIENTS

A PERSONAL MARKETING SYSTEM
FOR FINANCIAL PROFESSIONALS

DERRICK KINNEY

WILEY

John Wiley & Sons, Inc.

To my incredibly wise, loving, and supportive wife, Kara
and
my wonderful children, Lauren, Hannah, and Conner

Published by John Wiley & Sons, Inc., Hoboken, New Jersey.
Published simultaneously in Canada.

For general information on our other products and services, or technical support, please contact our Customer Care Department within the United States at 800-762-2974, outside the United States at 317-572-3993 or fax 317-572-4002.

Wiley also publishes its books in a variety of electronic formats. Some content that appears in print may not be available in electronic books.

For more information about Wiley products, visit our web site at www.wiley.com.

Library of Congress Cataloging-in-Publication Data
Kinney, Derrick.
  Master the media to attract your ideal clients : a personal marketing system for
  financial professionals / Derrick Kinney.
    p. cm.
"Published simultaneously in Canada."
Includes index.
  ISBN 0-471-48256-0 (cloth : alk. paper)
  1. Financial planners—Marketing. I. Title.
HG179.5 .K56 2004
332.024'0068'8—dc22

                                                                    2003026690

Printed in the United States of America.
10 9 8 7 6 5 4 3 2

CONTENTS

CHAPTER ONE

EXPLOIT YOUR STRENGTHS

Awakened from a deep sleep, Mary fumbled through the darkness to stop the incessant ringing of the alarm clock. "Another day, another dollar," she muttered groggily as she pulled herself out of bed. As she made her way to the kitchen to prepare her breakfast, Mary switched the television on and listened to the news anchors describing the events of the morning.

"And with more on this late-breaking financial story, we turn now to our financial expert," the anchor said, a sense of urgency in his voice. Wondering what had happened, Mary was glued to the television. The financial expert began to describe what had caused the sharp drop in the stock market the day before. He went on to explain calmly what this news meant to the average investor like her.

Over the years, this expert had become more than just someone reporting the financial news. He had become like a trusted friend to Mary, who always listened carefully to what the financial expert said and benefited from his timely and knowledgeable advice. He's always able to describe things in a way that really makes sense to me. We need to meet with him, Mary thought.

A few months later Mary finally made that call. She and her husband met with the financial expert, who designed a customized game plan to help them meet their financial goals. Mary and her husband told the expert that he was just as professional and trustworthy in person as he appeared on television. The expert couldn't help but laugh. Smiling, he remarked, "I hear that a lot lately." Now each time Mary sees their financial advisor on television or reads his quote in a news story, she displays a proud smile. It confirms that she and her husband made the right choice. They are pleased to refer others to the financial expert.

Each day the media seeks out financial services professionals to provide perspective on the day's financial events. Countless people just like Mary are looking for "an expert" to begin working with. There is no better time for financial professionals to establish themselves as the experts people can trust and turn to for timely financial information. Media contacts are searching for someone to help their audiences navigate the difficult financial environment. By consistently following a simple strategy, you can leverage free media exposure to gain visibility, enhance your credibility, and experience greater profitability. You can become the "financial expert" whom the media calls.

DO YOU HAVE WHAT IT TAKES?

Becoming known as an expert is not the same as being a one-shot media event. Instead, in this book you're going to learn the techniques and strategies of how to begin appearing in the media on a regular and frequent basis. And you'll get an up-close and personal look at how to immerse yourself into the media so that it becomes an invaluable part of your everyday business. In fact, you'll begin to wonder how you ever ran your business without utilizing this amazing marketing tool. This book will show you how to build maximum name recognition for yourself and to become the trusted expert in your community.

Being successful in the media takes a full commitment on your part. Think about your own role as a member of the audience or as a consumer. It takes a while for you to begin noticing people in the media, to begin remembering their names and really listening to what they say. Your own involvement in the media is no different—

it is not an overnight solution to raking in business. But, over time, if you stick with it and become good at it, you will reap the rewards.

Being in the media isn't for everyone. If you're not willing to arrive at the studio at the crack of dawn, have your schedule interrupted when a reporter calls, or stay on top of your field on a daily basis, you may want to consider other ways to grow your business. If, however, you realize that achieving anything great takes perseverance, then you have what it takes to experience success as a recognized expert and enjoy the massive exposure that only the media can deliver.

MEDIA ACTION POINTS

✔ Success in the media requires a 100 percent commitment on your part.

✔ Stay up-to-date in your field. Always know the latest financial news.

✔ Now is the time for *you* to be the financial expert!

LOCAL MEDIA RELATIONS CONNECTS ADVERTISING TO SALES

If you watch prime-time television, you're likely to see commercials for several different financial services and insurance companies. Why do they spend so much money on national advertising? To create awareness of their companies in the minds of viewers. These companies run commercials during specific shows because they know that, based on market research, the viewers they want as clients are watching those programs. They want to create positive exposure for their company. However, the problem with advertising is that it's often overlooked as clutter. Many times viewers change the channel or leave the room during commercials. While viewers may remember a certain commercial, product, or company, they don't necessarily feel inspired to go out and buy immediately. When people see a commercial for investments or insurance, in particular, they typically won't run to the phone book and call to set an appointment right then. The financial services business is a relationship business. People don't buy the commercial; they buy a relationship with a trusted advisor.

How can you capitalize on this national advertising? The answer lies in examining three principles of consumer psychology at work here.

Three Consumer Psychology Principles

Principle 1. Commercials don't trigger immediate financial services sales.

Principle 2. Financial relationships begin at the local level.

Principle 3. Purchasing decisions frequently are based on convenience.

The first principle is that most people don't run to the phone and set an appointment when they see a financial services commercial, just as they don't run out and buy any product or service immediately after seeing a commercial for it. For investment and insurance companies, the primary purpose of commercials is to build ongoing awareness of their products and services, in the hope that one day, when the need arises, viewers will choose to do business with that company.

The second principle is that a relationship with a financial professional is initiated primarily at the local level, where the prospective client lives or works. When it comes to their money, most people like to be able to shake hands and look into the eyes of the person they have hired to help them manage their hard-earned dollars. Ask yourself this question: Would you blindly invest your life savings with someone you've not met personally? Other investors are the same way. They don't want to invest their savings with a stranger. They want a personal relationship with a trusted financial professional. It's the same reason so many people do their banking inside the bank instead of using the drive-through or the ATM. They prefer the personal touch that only face-to-face interaction can provide.

The third principle is that most people purchase goods and services when the process is easy and the location is convenient for them. Many people feel inconvenienced if they have to drive more than 30 minutes to a financial professional's office. Whether people are going to the dry cleaner's or the doctor's, they don't want to waste a lot of time fighting traffic to get there.

These three principles of consumer psychology point to the fact that the majority of purchasing decisions for financial products are made at the local level. That's why a locally based media relations campaign is so critical if you want to accomplish a huge break-through in marketing to your local community. A local media cam-paign is the doorway that you build so that future clients can walk into your business. It's how you can tap into the power of national advertising and use it to generate tangible sales for you in your local buying area.

Table 1.1 illustrates the thought process of the average investor.

Since investors want to work with financial professionals on the local level, what's the best way for you to capitalize on this opportu-nity? It depends on whether you are an independent financial pro-fessional or are affiliated with a nationally recognized company.

If you are an independent advisor, here's the opportunity for you:

Because of the number of financial commercials people see, it's easy for investors to be confused. Since most companies sound sim-ilar, it can be difficult for people to differentiate between them. That's where you come in. Because you must resolve people's con-fusion, your appearances in the local media become even more crit-ical. For you, the media is a way to differentiate yourself in a very

Table 1.1 How Investors Respond to Advertising

Financial Firm Action	Investor Reaction
National advertising	"Hmmm, another commercial for a financial firm. This is all so confusing. They all sound the same. How can I cut through the clutter?"
Local media	"That advisor explains things in a way that makes sense, and I like his style. Plus, he's in my local area. I'll contact him."
Sales	"This advisor is just as professional and knowledgeable in person as he is in the media. I'll invest with him."

crowded marketplace. Because you don't have the advantage of a company that advertises nationally, you have to be even more thoughtful and creative in generating awareness for yourself and your company.

When you appear in the media, your competitive angle should be: "I'm independent and proud of it. I'm not tied to any one company, so I have an unbiased view of your investment opportunities. I recommend that you work with an independent financial professional."

If your company does national advertising, here's the opportunity you have:

National advertising creates awareness of your company. When you appear in your local media, you are directly connecting your national company to you, the qualified financial expert on the local level. Often a prospect wants to invest with your company but isn't sure whom to contact locally. As you begin appearing in the local media, and as that investor begins to notice you, it's likely that he or she will call you when the need arises. This process directly connects national advertising to tangible sales for you and your company.

When you appear in the media, your competitive angle should be: "I am a financial professional who is associated with a nationally recognized company. I find most investors prefer the security of working with a company with a strong brand name."

Here's the main point: Regardless of how your business is set up, whether you're independent or affiliated with a national company, the key is to make a conscious decision that you are going to be the financial professional of choice in your local buying area. If you market yourself successfully, clients with money will be drawn to you. As you begin to appear in the media, you must realize that the only limitations you have will be those that you place on yourself. It's all about marketing!

BE THE NEWS

As a financial professional, when you appear in the media, you're part of the news, not an advertisement. That's the beauty of putting effective media relations into practice. Plus, a media relations campaign can be conducted at a fraction of the cost of paid advertising—and is usually more effective. This doesn't mean that a media campaign is destined to make you an immediate profit. The goal of media relations is to build not only name recognition but also trust. With each appearance in the media, you are building credibility in the eyes of your audience, and you are increasing the likelihood that its members will call on you when they need financial advice. You're also distancing yourself further from your competition. At the same time as other financial professionals out there are making unsolicited attempts to reach prospects, those same prospects are seeing and hearing you as the financial expert in the media.

You must place yourself on the offensive and position yourself to begin attracting the clients you want. As a natural consequence of acquiring more new clients, you'll become more profitable and have a lot more fun. Although your results may not be immediate, you'll be sowing the seeds in the minds of your future clients. Over time, those seeds will grow. When a triggering event occurs in their lives that makes them realize that they need a qualified financial professional, you will have positioned yourself to be their natural choice.

THE MEDIA MULTIPLIER

Would you rather have to say the same message 1,000 times, or say it once and have it heard by 1,000 people? It's easy to figure out which is a better use of your time. Consider this for a moment: How long would it take you physically to meet with 1,000 people? If you met with each person for only 30 minutes, for eight hours a day, five days a week, it would take you over three months. Now, that's a daunting task. But if you appear as a guest on television or on a radio newscast, or if you're interviewed in an article for a newspaper or financial web site, you can reach that many people easily in just three to four minutes each time. And truth be told, the numbers typically are far greater than that—sometimes you're reaching tens of thousands or hundreds of thousands of prospective clients with each interview that you do. Media access offers you a huge opportunity to take your message to countless ideal clients at one time.

Marketing research indicates that people need to see a person's name or a company name 8 to 10 times before they begin to recognize and remember it consciously. In the financial services business, often we are taught to use what is referred to as "drip marketing" in order to overcome this problem. Drip marketing can involve mailing or e-mailing to a certain group of prospective clients every month for a year or more, so that you're "dripping" your key marketing messages on them. The goal is that, over time, the recipients of your information will begin to recognize your name and decide to use your services at some point in the future. This same concept works with the media audience. The more often people see or hear your name and company name, the more familiar they become with you. And the more quickly they develop a favorable impression of you and your business.

One of the things I hear from many financial professionals is that they feel they are working too hard for too little money. And not only are they struggling financially, but they feel they're spending too much time away from their families. They feel trapped and they don't know what to do to change it. I have good news for you. It's time for that to change! As you begin to generate more business due to your media appearances, you'll be putting yourself in a position to impact your quality of life significantly. Since the media allows you to market yourself effectively to many people in a short amount of time, you'll begin to find that you're getting more done in much less time than it used to take and you're making more money. You'll be faced with choosing how you want to spend all the extra time you now have.

Effective media coverage gives you two options:

1. Make the same amount of money in less time. Because you're attracting more of the clients you want more quickly, you can choose to keep your income level. But now you have the freedom in your schedule to spend more time with your family or doing what you enjoy.

2. Make more money in the same amount of time. You already have your business engine running on all cylinders. When you add media appearances to your existing marketing plan of attack, you can experience a significant breakthrough in the number of new clients you acquire and the income you bring home.

The choice is yours: Make the same amount of money or make much more money. You get to select which option lets you achieve the quality of life that's best for you. Clearly, the media allow you to convey your message efficiently, in a way that lets you work smarter, not harder.

WHAT ARE YOUR STRENGTHS?

Do you ever wonder why some people always seem to be successful at what they do? It seems as if everything they touch turns to gold. Every day in the business world, there is news of another person achieving great things. Are some people just born lucky? Or is it pure coincidence that some people hit the big time while others feel they're always running out of time?

In my experience, I've found that successful people consistently place themselves in a position to be successful. It's not by accident—it's by design. They may not achieve their goal the first time, or even the second time. But with laser precision, they repeatedly place themselves in a position to reap the rewards they're seeking. So when an opportunity presents itself, there they are, prepared to reach out and seize success for themselves.

How do these people obtain success? By exploiting their strengths. They uncover their unique strengths—what sets them apart and what they excel at—and they capitalize on those strengths. When you consciously place yourself in the media, you are putting yourself in prime position for good things to happen. And not just now, but far into the future. This is the key to success in the media and in your overall business, and this is what you're about to learn.

In order to be successful in the media, you need to discover which aspects of the media you feel most comfortable with. It may be one or two of the media outlets. Or you may be able to handle all the various media outlets with ease. Whatever your situation, typically you'll discover one media outlet that you most enjoy and you feel really showcases your ability to communicate effectively with your target audience. Your personality may be best suited for the television camera. You may have a resounding voice and be drawn to radio. Or you may determine that your ideas are best expressed in writing. The questions in the media action points box will help you uncover your strengths and reveal the media outlets for which you may be best suited. The purpose of this exercise is twofold.

1. These questions will help you identify the media category that you may enjoy the most.

2. More important, the exercise will help you identify which media categories make you feel most uncomfortable and nervous. Remember, it's better for you not to have appeared in the media at all than to come across shaken and disoriented on the air or to submit a poorly written guest article to your local paper instead of making a strong first impression.

MEDIA ACTION POINTS

To identify your strengths, answer these questions:

✔ What tasks do you enjoy most about your current job?

✔ What tasks do you least enjoy about your current job?

✔ Do you enjoy being in front of people? Why or why not?

✔ Do you speak well? How do you know?

✔ Do you enjoy writing? Are you good at it?

✔ When you need to speak to someone, do you prefer to call, write an e-mail, or see the person face-to-face? Which type of communication are you most confident using?

✔ Do you get nervous being in front of people?

✔ What would other people say is your strength in communicating?

✔ What is your least favorite way to communicate?

Review your answers to these questions and determine which media outlet you find yourself drawn to. If you enjoy communicating face-to-face and in front of people, you may be headed for television. If you communicate best by phone, radio may be a good fit.

And if you prefer to send e-mails to people or to write letters, then the print media may be the path to follow. The key is to focus your media energies where you are most comfortable and have the highest probability of positioning yourself for success. Use this new-found information about yourself to prioritize your media game plan and focus your energies on what you do best.

WHAT IS YOUR COMMUNICATION STYLE?

Another component of positioning yourself to be successful with the media is to appreciate and understand your unique style of communicating. Watch or listen to the national and local news anchors. Each of them has a unique style, from how they speak to the mannerisms they use. As you study them carefully, you'll begin to see how well they paint a picture with their words. The good news is that you can use the same methods they do to be successful in communicating.

In media relations, there are two primary levels of communication, the fundamental and the personal, as shown in Table 1.2.

How well do you communicate on these two levels? Evaluate yourself now, based on what you know about yourself from your experiences in speaking both publicly and informally. Television and radio producers aren't just looking for people to speak about a topic. What they really want is someone who will captivate their viewers and listeners with thought-provoking and timely information.

Table 1.2 Two Forms of Communicating with the Media

LEVEL 1: The Fundamental (Minimum expectations of all speakers)	LEVEL 2: The Personal (Attributes that define the uniqueness of each speaker)
• Has knowledge of the topic • Speaks clearly and enunciates well • Conveys confidence	• Effectively varies vocal pitch • Uses mannerisms to emphasize key points • Speaks authoritatively

That's what increases their audience, drives up their ratings, and sells more advertising. When you appear in the media, the key is to emulate, not to imitate. No one wants to see a carbon copy of another guest. So continue to critique your media appearances and work to improve each time. Remember that you are unique. The quickest way for you to experience success in the media is by leveraging your special talents in communicating.

Think of star athletes. On game day, they don't succeed simply by running onto the field with no preparation or strategy. They watch their game films to critique themselves on the good and bad things they've done in the past so they can show significant improvement the next time they compete. Elite athletes take it a step further. They study how other star athletes play their position so they can improve their own performances. They aggressively search for every angle to gain an advantage over their competition. Each time you appear on television or radio, record it so you can go back and analyze your interview "game tape." Have someone else review the tape with you to pick up on even the slightest area for improvement. Let's be honest here. Watching and listening to yourself over and over can be a bit unnerving. But believe me, it is the best way to truly see what the audience sees. As you're getting started, media interviews can be hard to come by, so you need to execute and then study each of your appearances with the intensity of an athlete.

What's the quickest way for you to improve your interview skills? Follow this simple system: Do your first interview, then critique yourself strictly, and then quickly do another interview. As you begin to be interviewed more frequently, continue to implement this system to spot-check your performances. Think of this process as a cram course on media interviewing skills. Save a copy of every interview you do for a newspaper or magazine to see how closely the reporter captured your comments and the key points you were trying to convey. Think back to when you spoke to the reporter. Try to recall exactly what you said when you were answering the questions. Did the reporter quote you accurately, or were your comments taken out of context? Decide now what you'll do differently the next time a reporter calls you for an interview.

Use this checklist when reviewing your television interviews:

TV Interview Critique Checklist

❑ Did you speak too quickly or too slowly?

❑ How does your voice sound—smooth and relaxed, or nervous?

❑ Did you sit up straight, or do you appear to be slouching?

❑ Do you appear relaxed in your body language?

❑ Did you smile periodically?

❑ Did you use the anchor's name as you answered some of the questions?

❑ Did you appear to know what you were talking about?

❑ Did you use simple language (not industry jargon) to make your points?

❑ On a scale of 1 to 10 ("1" being poor, "10" being excellent), how would you rate the interview?

❑ What would you change for your next interview?

Use this checklist when reviewing your radio interviews:

Radio Interview Critique Checklist

❑ Did you speak too quickly or too slowly?

❑ How does your voice sound—smooth and relaxed or nervous?

❑ Did you smile periodically? (Note: Smiles can be heard in your voice inflection.)

❑ Did you use the anchor's name as you answered some of the questions?

❑ Did you sound as if you knew what you were talking about?

❑ Did you use simple language (not industry jargon) to make your points?

❑ On a scale of 1 to 10 ("1" being poor, "10" being excellent), how would you rate the interview?

❑ What would you change for your next interview?

Here's a checklist to review what you were quoted as saying in a newspaper, magazine, or other print media:

Newspaper Interview Critique Checklist

❏ Did the reporter accurately report your comments?

❏ Did you sound as if you knew what you were talking about?

❏ Were your name, title, and company name printed correctly?

❏ Did you use simple language (not industry jargon) to make your points?

❏ On a scale of 1 to 10 ("1" being poor, "10" being excellent), how would you rate the interview?

❏ What would you change for your next interview?

PERFECTING YOUR COMMUNICATION STYLE

The more you work with the media and the more comfortable you become with speaking, the more confident you will become in your abilities. If you appear in the media only sporadically, it can be difficult to improve on each interview because you're not doing it enough—especially if you're being interviewed every few weeks. In order to maintain a level of continuity, it's important to continually practice being interviewed.

The more critically you evaluate your performance, the better your chances of improving the next time. Just as in any sports activity, the more you practice and refine your skills, the better you feel about playing and the better results you start to see. As the saying goes, "Practice makes perfect." Working with the media is the same way. Take it very seriously. Study other people who are being interviewed. Learn from them and implement into your routine what you see them doing well, and you'll begin to see more and more media outlets call on you.

MEDIA ACTION POINTS

✔ Each time you appear in the media, carefully critique yourself. Improve on the small details.

✔ Focus your attention on speaking clearly.

✔ With each interview you do, you will feel more confident.

✔ Set a goal of doing a certain number of interviews each month.

CREATE YOUR PLAN FOR SUCCESS

Here are the three key factors to consider in creating your plan for media success:

1. Speak or write on what you know.
2. Focus on the media category that best showcases your strengths.
3. Target the specific media outlets that your ideal client is tuned in to.

Remember this essential rule regarding appearing in the media: Speak or write only on what you know. If a media opportunity comes your way that is not completely in line with your expertise, don't accept. Refer the appearance to someone else who is an expert in that area. Let's face it, you'll be tempted to accept the opportunity. You may tell yourself that you can fake your way through the interview just to get the media exposure. But the potential downside is too great. What if you get asked a question to which you don't know the answer? What would you do? You've seen others have the deer-in-the-headlights look, but now you'll be the one who feels trapped.

The other pitfall to speaking on topics outside your field is that doing so can dilute your effectiveness as a professional. Think of it this way: If you were in need of a delicate medical procedure, would you rather have the general practitioner or the renowned specialist conduct the surgery? The same holds true in the media. Media outlets always want the best expert they can find. But they don't always know who the expert is. Then you have a shared responsibility. If you are an expert on the topic, take the opportunity and do the interview. If, however, you sense that a media opportunity is outside the scope of your expertise and knowledge, simply say: "My expertise is in topic X, so it's probably best if I don't comment on that. But I know someone who does specialize in that area, and I can refer you." Then give the reporter the name and number of your contact to make it very easy for the media to contact that person. By doing so, you'll enhance your own credibility with the media representatives, and you'll become a key contact for future calls. When the need arises, they'll call you because they know that you'll be honest about whether you are the best person for the interview or whether another expert might be. And what a great position that is to be in—having the media call you with all requests related to finances. You become an interview gatekeeper, choosing which interviews to take and forwarding the others to appreciative professionals.

The second aspect of your plan to experience success in the media is to determine the media category on which you should focus your primary attention. Initially, any media exposure is good media exposure. However, over time, it will be critical to find the media outlet where you are most comfortable. To exploit your strengths fully, you must discover what you enjoy doing and capitalize on it by positioning yourself in the media outlet that best utilizes those strengths.

Table 1.3 provides a list of the major media categories to select from.

Use Table 1.3 to brainstorm the various media channels in your community. Follow these steps:

1. Circle the media category you feel you're best suited for, based on the questions you answered earlier.

2. Review the list of media outlets, and determine which ones may present an opportunity in your area.

Table 1.3   Media Category Matrix

Media Categories	Media Outlets	Local Media Outlets
Television	• National news programs • Local news programs • Cable-access news programs	Bloomberg, CNN, CNBC ABC, NBC, CBS, FOX, UPN, WB affiliates Check your local cable listings
Radio	• Nationally syndicated programs • National news programs • Local news programs • Local music stations	Bloomberg Radio National Public Radio Check your local radio listings
Newspapers/ Magazines	• National newspapers • Local newspapers • Local business newspapers • National trade publications • Company/community newsletters	*USA Today, Wall St. Journal* *Chicago Tribune* *Crain's NY Business* *Money, Forbes, Barron's* Check with large companies in your local area.
Internet	• National financial news pages • Local web content	MSN.com, CBS Marketwatch.com, cnnmoney.com Check your local media web sites

3. Write down the local media outlets you can contact about becoming a financial source for their stories.

The third part of your marketing plan is to determine which of these channels your ideal prospects are tuning in to. Think back to earlier in the chapter, when you answered the questions about defining who you are. Now let's take that same approach to developing your maximum media relations plan of attack. Think about each of the questions in the Media Action Points box and answer them carefully. All of these questions may not apply to your situation.

MEDIA ACTION POINTS

✔ What is the one characteristic that makes you and your business unique?

✔ Define your ideal client (age, minimum investment levels, income levels, specific industries, etc.).

✔ List three clients you have now who fit in the "ideal" category.

✔ How did they become your clients?

✔ What media outlets would best reach your ideal clients?

✔ Which of your strengths could be leveraged into media activities to attract more people in the "ideal" category?

Many financial professionals I talk with don't have a clear picture of the typical "average" client in their current client database. For this reason, it's helpful to complete a spreadsheet like the one in Table 1.4 to identify the types of clients you are attracting now. Once you evaluate the client data in your situation, you will have tangible information on which to base your marketing decisions. After evaluating the information about your current clients, you may discover that you are reaching exactly the type of clients you want. Or you may determine that the level of clients you are working with is not profitable for you. You further may discover that you need to shift your strategy radically to begin attracting a completely different type of client.

By answering the Media Action Points questions and completing the Ideal Client Profile, you should be able to focus your strengths and develop a marketing plan that will impact and reach your ideal prospects. Once you have a handle on who your ideal prospects are, one of the best ways to determine which media they use is to call each station, newspaper, or magazine and ask for a demographic report of their audience. Then, based on the information in those reports, you can determine which channels are ideal for your message.

The bottom line in creating your media plan is to find what you absolutely enjoy and then work it to perfection. By doing so, you'll

Table 1.4 Ideal Client Profile

Client Name	Age	Total Assets Invested	Title	Company

How Client Was Acquired	Average Age	Average Total Assets	Occupational Classes	Specific Companies

not only project yourself and your company in a way that accurately reflects who you are and what you enjoy doing, but you'll also help drive your business to the top. Most important, you'll begin to consistently attract the ideal clients you've always wanted but you didn't know how to reach.

MAXIMIZING THE MEDIA

Once you've identified your strengths, you can begin to leverage them to achieve massive marketing exposure for you and your business. Whether you're an independent advisor, work for a large financial services company, or run an accounting firm, maximizing your media exposure is critical to achieving a breakthrough for your business.

In sales, the goal is to generate the most revenue and grow the company's market share to number one. In effective media relations, the purpose is to build "mind share" among prospective clients and become their number-one choice for a financial professional. Building mind share is about creating and nurturing positive messages about you and your company in prospective clients' minds, messages that will lead them to buy from you in the future.

No longer should you be satisfied with a shotgun approach to marketing that claims that any marketing is good marketing. That idea is absolutely false. Remember this key point: The most successful people and businesses capture the minds and hearts of their customers with a powerful, authentic message. They repeat the same key messages over and over again until their ideal clients can't help but notice them and accept them. Once you've captured your prospective customers in this way, they will consider themselves to be your clients *before* they actually buy from you. This is an intriguing phenomenon. As you appear in the media on a regular basis, your name will become so embedded in your prospects' minds that as soon as they feel the need for your product or service, they will not even think of calling anyone but you. That is the result of maximizing the media.

Let me share with you a personal story. I appear in my local media on a weekly basis. Here is what I have found to be one of the keys to achieving success and attracting my ideal clients: I work to convey an authentic message and do it on a consistent basis. Prospective clients who call my office to schedule an appointment frequently tell me and my staff that they appreciate my down-to-earth approach and feel like they already know me. When I started my work in the media and this first began to happen, I didn't think much about it. However, over time, I began to see a pattern unfolding. People would see me on television. Then they would call to set up an appointment to discuss handling their investments and insurance. In most cases, their accounts were quite sizable, and they fit my ideal client profile. It was becoming that simple.

I realized that the media was a powerful tool I could use to reach my ideal clients and achieve my income and business goals. But more important, I discovered that the tremendous media exposure I was getting allowed me to "presell" myself before prospective clients even walked in my door. These ideal clients had already decided to work with me before they came into my office. All that was left was for me to do was to decide if I wanted to take them on as clients. However, the more I thought about this amazing concept, I realized that I had been leaving the results of my media exposure to total chance. I was doing interviews that got my name in the paper or my face on television, but I wasn't harnessing fully the vast power of this incredible marketing machine. From that point on, I went on the offensive and began to take control of my marketing destiny. I began selecting topics for my interviews that would hone in on my ideal clients like a laser beam and cause even more of them to contact me to set up an appointment. When newspapers called me, I began incorporating phrases into my answers that would grab the interest of a preretired or retired investor (my target market).

By implementing the strategies in this book, you too can experience the joy of having your ideal clients choose to work with you even before they even arrive at your office. You'll have them asking *you* to work with them!

This is the idea behind the "Maximizing the Media" continuum shown in Figure 1.1.

The first section of the graph represents people who become *aware* of your message for the first time. The middle section represents the people who have heard and seen your message enough to

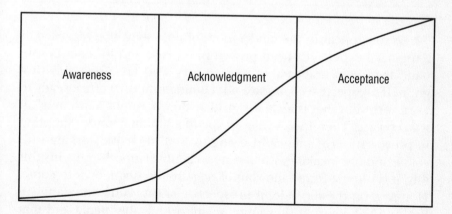

Figure 1.1 Media Marketing Continuum

at least *acknowledge* that they've seen or heard you before. On the far right are the people who have seen or heard you so many times, they not only recognize you but also completely *accept* what you are saying. Remember, these people have not done any business with you yet. But because they have heard and seen you so much in the media, they *will* do business with you when the need arises. Interestingly enough, when potential clients are in the far right end of the "Maximizing the Media" continuum, in their minds they actually consider you to be the one from whom they are already buying—even before they have purchased any financial products from you. When this happens, you have succeeded in your goal of building mind share with these prospective clients.

MEDIA ACTION POINTS

Answer these questions to help determine where you think you and your company are on the "Maximizing the Media" continuum.

✔ When prospective clients come into your office, do they tell you that they see or hear you in the media?

✔ Are prospective clients prepared to begin working with you now, or are they just shopping around?

✔ Do you spend a lot time convincing prospective clients to work with you?

As you appear in the media more often, you will be regarded as a financial expert. It's been proven in my case and for countless financial professionals across the country who are using this program. If prospective clients are not coming into your office ready to work with you, that is a clear sign that they have no "awareness" of who you are. Therefore, you must spend additional time attempting to prove your credibility and trying to "sell" them on working with you. Candidly speaking, when a new client relationship begins this way, it is often a foreshadowing of negative consequences to come. However, on the flip side, if prospective clients come into your office and tell you that they enjoy seeing you in the media and that they hope you can help them, it's a clear indication that they have accepted you as their financial professional. This is the place on the "Maximizing the Media" continuum that you should aspire to.

Place an "x" on the continuum in Figure 1.1 where you feel people's perception is of you and your company right now. Use this as a starting point for where to begin your media initiatives.

I realize that each person reading this book is at a different point in terms of experience with the media. You may have been interviewed many times, or you may have purchased this book so you could start your media journey and begin tapping in to the many benefits that media exposure can provide you. Whatever your experience, the key is to draw a line in the sand right now that signifies a new starting point in your media initiatives and in how you market yourself and your business. That line means that you will not pat yourself on the back for just having read this book. Instead, you will commit to implement these strategies for success. Will you accept the challenge?

---

30 Days to Creating a Marketing Mentality

Read this statement aloud every day for 30 days so it becomes a habit and a new way of positive business thinking for you.

Today I choose to take control of how I market myself. It is my daily responsibility to seek out new and exciting opportunities to create massive exposure for me and my business. I am confident and knowledgeable, and there is no better financial professional for ideal clients to work with than me. The only limitations I face are the ones I imagine in my own mind. Today I will be brave and courageous and step outside of the comfort zone that has held me captive for too long. Today I choose to be successful and accomplish great things.

Truly harnessing your energies in the media requires you to believe firmly that marketing is 100% your responsibility. No one can do it for you. And no one can have the same passion about your marketing than you. Remember: To maximize the media, you must exploit your strengths. Maximum marketing is about generating *high-impact exposure* for you and your company with *low-impact effort.* Media outlets allow you to multiply yourself and your message.

As you're establishing yourself in the media, you must ensure that what you're doing genuinely reflects who you are and creates an accurate image of that genuine self. There is nothing worse than creating an image of yourself that is not you, just for the sake of making money. You don't want to become known as the sleazy "used car pitchman" of your profession. When you're meeting with new clients and they mention they saw you on television or that they see you in the newspaper all the time, the person they see in the media should be the same person they are talking to. You must come across as the same knowledgeable, trustworthy, and down-to-earth person when they meet you in your office. This helps to further cement in their minds that they are making a good decision to begin working with you.

RECOGNIZE THE STRENGTH OF THE MEDIA

Remember, your media relationship is a two-way street. Always focus on giving your media contacts what they want, when they want it. Then you'll get exactly what you want: more new clients, more money, and the steady stream of business you've always wanted. When you appear in the media, you are being placed before their vast audience with an implied endorsement of your credentials and ability. The outlets have selected you because they believe you possess the information and the skills to communicate effectively with their audience. When your media contacts say "jump," you need to ask "how high?" and then jump even higher. Remember, it's not about your needs. It's always about the media outlets' needs. Realize that, and you will have the opportunity to be wildly successful. Your exposure (and, ultimately, the additional clients that you'll receive) is secondary to the media outlets getting what they want.

As you become more and more media savvy, and as people begin to comment on your interviews, constantly remind yourself where your media opportunities have come from and nurture those relationships. Never bite the hand that feeds you. And always try to avoid saying "no" to a media opportunity. Often media outlets operate on a last-minute, interrupted schedule, and they expect for you to do the same by putting their needs above yours. Being a team player with the media is well worth the work. Always have the attitude that your media opportunities are a gift—and a gift that the media reserve the right to exchange at any moment. Always give them your very best.

Realistically, you'll rarely have to drop everything to do an interview. But starting today, you must be comfortable with the fact that for you truly to leverage the media to help you achieve your goals, you must place the work you do in the media as a top priority. Let me shoot straight with you. As you begin to appear in the media more frequently, there will be times when a television or newspaper interview may interfere with your schedule. The bad news is that you may have to reschedule a client appointment, cause a client to wait a little longer in your lobby, wake up early to get to the news station, or otherwise disrupt your schedule. But the good news is that for all this "inconvenience" on your part, you are having the opportunity to experience powerful marketing exposure that other financial professionals only dream about. Plus, the media will remember your commitment to them. And that means more appearances and interviews for you!

EVERY INTERVIEW IS A FIRST IMPRESSION

Do you remember when you went on your first job interview? You looked your best, you said the right things, and your goal was to make a positive, lasting impression so you would be the one who got the job offer. It's the same way with the media. What's the best way to be successful in the media? Treat each interview you do as the only interview you'll ever do. You want that media outlet to hire you again and to be in front of its audience again. Always approach each interview with a mind-set for success. As they say in sports, "It's time for you to put your game face on." When a reporter calls you and begins asking you questions for the newspaper article she is writing, focus intently on the phone call and then give insightful answers that she will want to print. When a news anchor asks for your analysis on a financial issue, give an answer with unwavering focus and thoughtfulness. Put everything else in your mind aside and devote all your attention to the media.

With every interview you do, that particular media outlet's producers and editors are forming opinions about whether to invite you back to appear before their vast audience. Just like a coach watching game film, they're assessing how well you break down complex financial topics into easy-to-understand ideas. They're evaluating whether you are helping them get better or worse. More important, they're reviewing your information and approach to ensure it is providing a real service to their audience. Just as you did in your very first job interview, put yourself in the position where the media producers and editors want to "hire" you every day to deliver value to their audiences.

TREAT THE MEDIA LIKE A BUSINESS

Do some quick research into how Fortune 500 companies are run across the country, and you'll find that each corporation has specific goals it wants to accomplish each year. Typically those goals include increasing sales and revenue, growing market share, cutting costs, and becoming more efficient and effective. Media outlets operate in the exact same way. First and foremost, they are businesses—and fiercely competitive businesses at that. Throughout the year, each media outlet is ranked by its respective audience. During these ratings periods, television and radio stations fight tooth and nail to come out on top and be crowned the champion with the most market share. The media outlets that earn the highest numbers then can translate those numbers into higher advertising revenues, more viewers, and bragging rights. These are the most critical times of the year for all media outlets. For this reason, at these times the media outlets focus on bringing in guests they know will cause their audience to watch or listen.

Every time that you appear in the media, you're doing much more than just a simple interview. You're making a conscious decision to move forward or backward in your media career. And you're proving again and again to that media outlet that you are its best choice for a financial expert. Let me give you an example. When you're self-employed, it's up to you to hire the best possible people to help you run your company and accomplish your goals. In many cases, it's only after you've actually hired people that you really begin to find out about their work ethic and how productive they are. Over time, you'll find that employees exhibit one of two mind-sets: Either they think like a business owner or they think like an employee. Table 1.5 contrasts the attitudes of these types of employees.

When you work with the media, it's vital for you to exhibit a business owner mentality. With each interview that you do, your mind-set should be that what you say and do is absolutely critical to the long-term success of that particular media outlet. By intentionally having this mind-set, you will be more focused and effective in each interview. Personally, I approach all the media work I do with the seriousness and focus of a full-time job. When I walk through the doors of the television station to do my segment, I recognize that I no longer work for myself. Rather, I know that my boss at that moment is the station manager, my producer, my director, and the intern who is helping write my interview questions. And my sole purpose at that moment is to deliver financial information to viewers in a way that captures their attention and provides them with tangible assistance so they can make better financial decisions. My mind-set is that I am personally responsible for the success of this station and that I am going to do what I can to make my interview the best it possibly can be.

Having an employee mind-set can bring a promising future in the media to a screeching halt. I've done hundreds of interviews. And in that time, I have had the opportunity to meet many famous people who were also being interviewed. They've ranged from movie stars and sports figures to business leaders. It's interesting to get to meet them and visit with them for a few minutes. I have discovered that many of these "stars" expect the media to wait on them hand and foot.

Table 1.5 Inside the Mind of the Business Owner

Business Owner Mentality	Employee Mentality
• "I own it."	• "I just do what I am told."
• "It's up to me to make a difference."	• "I just want to get through the day. Is it five o'clock yet?"
• "The work I do is critical to helping this company reach its goals."	• "The work I do is 'busy work.' Who really cares about it?"
• "What can I do for the company?"	• "What can the company do for me?"

As a matter of fact, I often hear producers complaining about how demanding and "high-maintenance" some of these guests can be. These stars get invited to appear because the public is fascinated with them, and their appearances boost station ratings. But from what producers tell me, if it were up to them, they wouldn't invite many of these famous people back because of how difficult they are to work with. However, I was pleasantly surprised one day when I arrived at the TV studio for an interview. There sat sales guru and world-renowned motivational speaker Zig Ziglar, patiently waiting to go on the set for his interview. He had arrived early and spent a lot of time visiting with us in the waiting room. But what stood out the most to me was what the producers said about him after he left. They all commented on how nice he was and how enjoyable he was to work with. Zig Ziglar exemplified how to work perfectly with the media. Now, that's the way to get invited back happily! By giving the media outlets what they want, you can easily get what you want. Approach the media with the attitude that you are a team player and you want to contribute to the well-being of the organization. Doing so will help put you on the track to being invited back time and time again.

USE YOUR INTERNAL CLOCK

Each of us has a different time of day when we're most productive and effective—and when we're at our best. Some people like to get to the office early in the morning and start cranking out the work. They're highly focused, alert, and pride themselves on getting a lot done before most people even arrive at work. But there are many people who would like to rip the word "morning" right off the pages of their planners. At about the time the early risers are tiring, these night owls are just coming to life. These people are highly productive later in the day and are able to accomplish their key tasks late into the evening.

Remember this important point: Don't fight your internal clock. Instead, use it to your advantage. Examine yourself and determine when your best time of the day is and then structure your media time (and the rest of your schedule, for that matter) to capitalize on the time of day when you are most productive. This point is critical: If you're a morning person, target the morning news broadcasts or try to talk to reporters during the early part of the day. If you come to life in the afternoon or evening, focus your energies on media opportunities that occur late in the day. Personally, I'm a morning person. That's when I'm at my best. I try to get into the office early and hit the ground running. I'm able to be focused and alert at that time of the day. So it makes sense for me to focus my media efforts in the morning.

MEDIA ACTION POINTS

Here are three steps to leveraging your internal clock:

1. Evaluate yourself and determine when you're most productive.
2. Look at your calendar. See if client meetings or high-level business-building activities have fallen outside the time you're most highly productive.
3. Restructure your weekly calendar. Schedule your most profitable and important activities to fall inside your peak productivity time. That's when you're most likely to experience the greatest level of success.

Capitalizing on your internal clock is perhaps the most important aspect of playing to your strengths. Treat your body clock as your ally and not your enemy. Take full advantage of it and design your workweek so that you are doing the most dollar-productive activity when you're at your best.

Now, let's put this in perspective. There's a big difference between scheduled media appearances and those times when the media call you because of breaking financial news. Remember, to be successful in working with the media, you have to be flexible. As we discussed earlier, think of media coverage as a gift. Always respect that gift as if it were a rare, precious jewel. Your goal is to try to control as much of your media time as possible by scheduling it when you're at your best. However, when the media call, day or night, and they need you to comment on something for a news story or drive to the television or radio station to be interviewed, make every effort to drop what you're doing and go. By doing so, you'll reap the rewards for a long time to come.

PUT YOUR MEDIA GOALS IN YOUR CALENDAR

You've now identified your key strengths and the time of day when you're most productive and effective. It's time to begin setting some tangible, achievable media goals for yourself. I can hear you saying to yourself that you know all about goals. I'm sure you do, but how many of your goals have you actually achieved, and how many have gone unrealized? I'm going to show you how to increase significantly the probability that you'll achieve not only your media goals, but also your overall income and business goals. How? By reinforcing your goals through establishing a fixed weekly calendar, with "media follow-up time" blocked out in that calendar so you can't miss it. It's critical for you to set aside planned time each week to focus on your media efforts. Think of your media relationships as a beautiful garden. The garden must be fed, watered, and tended to on a regular basis.

So it is with breaking into the media. If you are going to be successful, you must make the activity of seeking media exposure a weekly habit. You need to make it a top priority for growing your business. The same theory that it takes 8 to 10 times for a person to begin to pay attention to something holds true for getting media attention. As you dedicate time to reaching your media contacts consistently and to creating the interview opportunities that I'll describe in later chapters, you'll begin seeing progress.

The best way to incorporate this media time into your schedule is to make a weekly fixed calendar, in which you attempt to repeat the same things at the same times each week. Examine what is working in your weekly calendar and what has been producing results for you. Then try to replicate those same activities week in and week out to create a predictable success pattern. The concept is simple: Keep doing the activities that are generating the results you want at the exact same times each week. By doing this, you don't have to keep reinventing the wheel—you don't have to rethink ways to create the same successful results you've experienced in the past. Then you can evaluate which actions are not generating positive outcomes for you.

Table 1.6 presents a sample fixed calendar.

Table 1.6 Weekly Fixed Calendar Template

Date: _____

Time	Monday	Tuesday	Wednesday	Thursday	Friday
8:00	Client appt:	Media follow-up time	Home with family	Out	Appt:
8:30	Client appt:				
9:00				Client Appt:	Client calls
9:30	TV appearance				
10:00		Client appt:			TV appearance
10:30	Client appt:				
11:00		Client appt:		Client appt:	Lunch
11:30	Client appt:				
12:00	Lunch	Lunch	Client appt:	Client appt:	Set weekly goals
12:30			Client appt:		
1:00	Weekly planning				
1:30	Client appt:	Client follow-up	Client follow-up	Client follow-up	Client follow-up
2:00					
2:30	Client appt:	Client appt:	Client appt:	Client appt:	Client appt:
3:00					
3:30	Client appt:	Client appt:	Client appt:	Client appt:	Client appt:
4:00					
4:30	Staff meeting	Staff meeting	Staff meeting	Staff meeting	Staff meeting
5:00	Leave office	Leave office	Leave office	Leave office	Leave office

Typical fixed calendar items are the critical tasks: phone calling, prospecting, client service, marketing, and the like. In addition to those key items, add "media follow-up time" to your calendar. This is the time you'll spend each week thinking of new ideas for your media appearances and pursuing more media opportunities. Also add to your fixed calendar client appointments each week, projects, and to-do items. This fixed calendar template can be re-created in any spreadsheet program.

PUT A SPENDING LIMIT ON YOUR TIME

Let me share with you a secret to increase your productivity significantly every day. Put time limits on everything you do. I talk with advisors all the time who tell me they plan on a client meeting lasting 30 minutes and it drags into 2 hours. Or they know, at the end of the day, that they've shuffled some papers around their desks, but they can't quite say that they truly accomplished anything significant that helped grow their businesses. No doubt, you've been the victim of such "time theft," and you've wondered where the time went and why you didn't get anything done. The key is for you to take control and begin to *own* your time. Treat it like a rare commodity.

As you fill in your weekly meetings and to-dos in your calendar, block out a fixed amount of time for each item. If you're going to meet with a client, decide ahead of time how long the meeting will last. When you go to the doctor's office, does she spend two hours with you? If she did, you might begin to wonder why she doesn't have other patients to see or why she's not busier. Don't let your clients think those things about you. People expect their financial expert to be very busy and to have a limited and structured amount of time in which to meet with clients.

Schedule 30-minute or 1-hour appointments with your clients. If you can't accomplish your goals in that much time, you should rethink how you're running your appointments. If your appointment is running long, simply say, "Well, we've accomplished a lot today. Let's go ahead and stop here." Then if you need to, meet with the client again the following week. This benefits you and the client because you're accomplishing more in less time. If you need to do some work for a client (run an investment report, design an insurance illustration, etc.), give yourself a fixed amount of time to accomplish the task. Doing so will cause you to be more focused and deliberate in getting the job done.

Financial professionals who have implemented this fixed calendar system tell me that their days now are filled with significant accomplishments. They leave the office each day feeling as if they made tangible progress toward their business goals. Working with this sense of urgency will allow you to run your client appointments more effectively and get your projects and to-do items accomplished in short order. The key is to custom-tailor your schedule based on your productivity pattern.

MEDIA ACTION POINTS

✔ Determine what time of day you are most productive.

✔ Fill in your key weekly tasks on your fixed calendar.

✔ Block out two hours per week (when you're at your best) for "media follow-up time."

✔ Schedule your time in fixed increments.

✔ Work with a sense of urgency.

✔ Put time limits on everything you do.

SET GOALS THAT STRETCH YOU

If you aren't setting goals and checking your progress often, the busyness of your daily life can overwhelm you. Each day will blend into the next until 10 or 20 years go by and you are left to wonder what you've accomplished. Write down your goals and put them in a place where you can look at them everyday—on the bathroom mirror, in your office, or by your bed. With the fast pace of life, it's very easy to forget what is not in front of you, demanding your attention. Make it a point to review your goals daily; doing so will give you more incentive to accomplish daily the key tasks that you need to do to help you get there.

Here's the easiest way to develop an action plan: Break down your yearly media goals into monthly goals, then weekly goals, then daily goals. For example, you may write that you want to appear on television at least once per month this year or write a guest article for the newspaper two times during the year. The simple action of setting goals and writing them down is powerful. Remember, setting goals doesn't guarantee you'll accomplish everything. But it allows you to make significant progress toward accomplishing what you would not have achieved if you didn't set the goals. Think of yourself as a rubber band and your goals as the fingers stretching you. The bigger the media goals you set, the more you'll be pulled. When your time frame for accomplishing the goal is over, whether you've hit it or not, you won't go back to your original shape because you've been stretched. And the next time you set a goal, you'll be that much closer to achieving it. Simply review your media goals once a week to keep them fresh in your mind.

MEDIA ACTION POINTS

Answer these questions to set your goals:

- ✔ What do you want to accomplish over the next 12 months in your business?
- ✔ What do you want to accomplish over the next 12 months in the media?
- ✔ What do you want to accomplish in 5 years in your business life?
- ✔ What do you want to accomplish in 5 years in your media plan?
- ✔ What do you want to accomplish in 10 years in your business life?
- ✔ What do you want to accomplish in 10 years in your media plan?

Take your goals seriously. The key to most people's success is related directly to goals they set for themselves. If you think big, then set big goals, and you will achieve big things with your media relations efforts. As Theodore Roosevelt so eloquently stated in 1910:

> It is not the critic who counts: not the man who points out how the strong man stumbles or where the doer of deeds could have done better. The credit belongs to the man who is actually in the arena, whose face is marred by dust and sweat and blood, who strives valiantly, who errs and comes up short again and again, because there is no effort without error or shortcoming, but who knows the great enthusiasms, the great devotions, who spends himself for a worthy cause; who, at the best, knows, in the end, the triumph of high achievement, and who, at the worst, if he fails, at least he fails while daring greatly, so that his place shall never be with those cold and timid souls who knew neither victory nor defeat.

Setting big goals for yourself today is the first step toward achieving long-term media success. Taking action to reach those goals will put you on the path to a magical marketing adventure.

CHALLENGE

As you discover your unique strengths and who your ideal clients are, you'll be taking the first steps toward creating your own special identity that will begin to revolutionize the way you think about marketing. Let the realization of your special talents and what you truly enjoy doing serve as the wind behind your back to push you to new heights in how you think about and run your business. If you implement the simple steps in this chapter and the chapters that follow, each and every day, you will move closer to your goal of becoming the recognized financial expert you always dreamed you could be. It's now within reach. With each chapter you complete, I challenge you to take action. Your media success story begins today. Read on and prepare for your next breakthrough.

CHAPTER TWO

BREAKING INTO THE MEDIA

The media are, collectively, a living, breathing organism that swarms to wherever news is breaking and to whatever people are most interested in at any given moment. One day it may be the last-minute touchdown that wins the championship for the home team. The next day it may a disaster that threatens the lives of thousands of people. Or it might be a breaking story on the economy or the stock market. Every day the media outlets put in the spotlight a new event, controversy, or person. What happened yesterday is old news. The media focus is on what is happening today and what it means to their audiences.

When you pick up a newspaper or turn on the evening news, you probably don't think much about the news that is reported. Most people take for granted the way the media identify what's newsworthy and what should be reported to their audiences. They view the media as reactive entities; events happen, and reporters simply relay the stories. At least, that's how it appears to the average person. However, operating invisible to the general public is a megamillion-dollar industry whose sole focus is to influence how and what is reported as news.

Welcome to the exciting world of public relations and media relations. Media relations firms are dedicated to brainstorming ideas

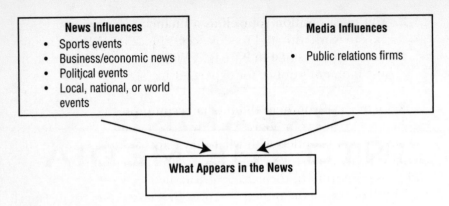

Figure 2.1 How News Is Influenced

proactively and searching for different news perspectives that will place their clients in the media. The media relations industry consists of independent media consultants, full-service media consulting firms, and in-house public relations offices at corporations and organizations. The primary purpose of this industry is to provide the media with news ideas and compelling story angles that put targeted companies, organizations, and clients in the best possible light. As you read on, you will discover how you can use those same techniques to place yourself in the news media in a proactive way—a way that places you inside of the news. See Figure 2.1.

In this chapter you'll learn how to implement a system of strategically and systematically contacting specific media contacts in your local area. You'll also learn how to begin pitching ideas to your local media contacts that will capture their attention and help you become the person they turn to when they need a financial expert.

HELP THE MEDIA AND THEY'LL HELP YOU

With all the newsworthy events that occur daily, how can you get your foot in the door to get noticed in the media? There are two basic steps:

1. You must differentiate yourself in a way that captures the media's attention.

2. You must position yourself as a financial professional who's easy to work with and readily accessible whenever the media call. Reporters like to have a list of advisors they can call on at a moment's notice for expert advice.

Remember, if you help the media accomplish their goals, they can help you reach your goals. As we discussed in the last chapter, as you supply media outlets with what they want for their viewers, the media can help meet your needs by routinely placing your name and picture in front of their expansive audiences.

Think of the media outlets as stores that constantly rotate their products to meet consumers' needs. As trends change, new products become more popular. Think of yourself as a potential product. If you want to succeed in the media's "marketplace," you have to sell well and make the store money. In order to do that, you have to appeal to the consumers and provide them with value, which in turn provides the store with value. In other words, if you want to appear in the media, you must present yourself as a specialty item from which they can profit. You must offer their audiences something of value that will make them watch you, listen to you, or read your words again and again.

Let's be honest. Your goal is to appear in the media for the tremendous exposure it offers. You want to be able to deliver a message once that can reach thousands of prospective clients. The media outlets want qualified and appealing guests or writers so that people continue to watch, listen, or read. Newspapers want to quote a variety of sources so they appear balanced in their reporting. The bottom line is that those in the media want to quote or interview the best possible experts so they can gain a higher share of their potential audience. Each media outlet wants its audience to feel confident that they are consistently hearing from the most timely and educated experts providing perspective on the day's news events. So appearing in the media is a two-way street—just don't let the media know that. When you begin working with the media, remember there is only one way: their way.

You must emphasize only how you can help the media accomplish their goals, not what they can do for you and your career. If you make any reference to how you will benefit from your exposure, you may appear self-serving and greedy and may miss out on an exciting opportunity. Instead, you want to position your media appearances as a valuable service you can provide to their audience that fills an existing void. That angle always wins with the media. Build the case with them that their audience has an unquenchable thirst for timely and relevant financial information. And that there is no better person to fill that void and meet that need than you. When you meet the media's need to provide the most timely and relevant information for their viewers, you achieve your goal of becoming a visible and credible source to your target market.

By appearing in the media, you are helping them get what they want—to inform their audience, stay ahead of their competition, and become the most popular source people turn to for critical information. Your primary role is continually to position yourself as a guest who helps the media achieve their goals. How do you do this? First, think of yourself as a business owner of the station, newspaper, or magazine in which you want to appear or be quoted. Business owners desperately want their businesses to succeed and grow. Simply put, businesses grow by selling more than their competition and by continually providing a better product than their competition. In the media's terms, if more people are tuned in to their programs or reading their publications, they can sell more advertising at a higher cost and they will continue to attract the largest audience. Business owners also have a constant need for feedback on how to make their business better. In Chapter Four you'll learn more about how to keep your media contacts happy and how to continue to provide them with quality story ideas and interview material.

When you appear in the media, it's important to remember that you work for two primary constituencies:

1. *The media outlet.* Imagine that you're a producer at a TV station. Things are changing minute by minute, and you have to keep up with it all. You're faced with one crisis after another, and it's up to you to help package the news in a way that both informs and appeals to your viewers. When you bring in local experts to provide perspective on the news of the day, you want guests who are knowledgeable. You also want these experts to be able to give you ideas on how to best

present the information to their audience. That would make your job easier. You'd want such guests to appear on your show on a regular basis, since they are helping you (the producer) achieve your goals.

2. *The media outlet's audience.* How do you work for an audience? By providing information in a way that is easy to understand and relevant. Financial institutions are notorious for making things sound more complicated than they need to be. For the average person, financial issues are confusing and can be difficult to grasp fully. You can shine by explaining complex financial topics in a way that makes sense to the average person. You'll know that what you're saying is coming across as uncomplicated if producers or reporters tell you that you have a way of discussing financial issues in a way that really makes sense to them. Remember this key point: You can't control the complexity of the news. You *can* control how you explain the relevance of the news to the average person.

By providing your media contacts with what they want, and by delivering an appealing and understandable perspective of the financial news to that media's audience, you will put yourself on the path to long-term success in the media.

MEDIA ACTION POINTS

✔ You can capture the media's attention by being sensitive to the needs of their audience.

✔ Being accessible to the media means more interview opportunities for you.

✔ Give your media contacts exactly what they want and you'll get what you want.

✔ Speak to the media in an easy-to-understand way.

RESEARCH THE MEDIA

Now that you understand your role with the media, it's time to begin researching the people you need to contact. First, go back to the two exercises you completed in Chapter One: "Identify Your Strengths" and the "Media Channels" chart. When you identified your strengths, you probably got a feel for which media format(s) is for you, whether it's television, radio, press, or the Internet. Now it's time to focus on one or two of those formats. You will launch your media campaign by contacting only people who work in those specific media outlets. However, if you feel comfortable appearing in all the different types of media outlets, expand your media campaign to include all media outlets. You always can narrow your contact list down the road.

Now think about the ideal clients whom you defined in Chapter One. Within your selected media format(s), which specific channels, programs, magazines, and so on would appeal to those clients? There are two ways to gather this information. You can talk to current clients who fit your "ideal" category, and ask them which programs they watch or listen to, what they read, and which Internet sites they use for information. Then tabulate the responses you get. Doing this will give you some nitty-gritty marketing research that you can use to make your decisions about where to focus your media energies. There's an old marketing story about how car washes advertised their services. Employees who drove the cars into the wash bay were instructed to write down the radio stations to which the dials were tuned. The car wash then would use that data to select which radio stations to advertise its services on. What an easy and effective way to do some marketing research on existing customers! Never underestimate the power of simply asking your ideal clients what their habits are, in order to help you identify ways to attract more people like them.

A second way for you to do your media research is to start contacting the specific programs, publications, and web sites you've identified and asking their marketing departments for demographic reports on their audiences. Demographic reports provide information on the age group targeted, average household income, and the estimated size of the audience at different times of day. In just a moment you'll begin using this information to narrow down your list of potential channels to those that appeal to the ideal prospects you want to attract.

In order to put these two pieces together—the media formats you're comfortable with and the channels that appeal to your target audience—fill out a chart like the one in Table 2.1. Under "Local Media Outlets," fill in the specific television or radio stations, newspapers or magazines, and web sites you've researched. Next to each of those outlets fill in the target audience. Again, you can get this information from the outlets themselves, either by looking at their web sites or by asking for a demographic report. Based on each outlet's target market, determine whether it's a fit with the ideal clients you want to reach.

Once you've filled out this chart and know which specific programs, publications, and sites you want to pursue, it's time to begin researching the specific contact people at each outlet. You'll want to look for these people: producers, editors, talent coordinators, and reporters. The information you need, at a minimum, is a name, a title, and a way to contact each person specifically, whether that's a fax number or an e-mail address. Don't settle for just a phone number, since you are going to be sending things to these people in writing.

How do you get this information? There are several options. The easiest way to begin is to go to the web site of each program or publication you want to get contacts for and search for a list. Often news programs provide a list of reporters. If you click on their names, you'll see biographies and e-mail addresses you can use to contact them with questions or story ideas. It is more difficult to get information for larger, national programs, but these shows often list a specific person's contact information for story ideas or a contact name for potential guests. Publications often list reporters and each person's field of expertise. Look through the list and select the names of those people who report specifically on personal finance, the economy, and your areas of expertise.

Table 2.1 How News Is Influenced

Media Format	Local Media Outlets	Target Audience	Fit?
Television			
Radio			
Print			
Internet			

HOW TO IDENTIFY
YOUR LOCAL MEDIA OUTLETS

Now it's time for you to utilize the incredible power of the Internet to launch your media campaign. Simply follow these four steps.

Step 1. Go to your favorite Internet search engine and type in any of these keywords/phrases:

- "(your city), (your state) media" For example: "Boston, MA media"
- "(your city), (your state) newspapers"
- "(your city), (your state) tv stations"
- "(your city), (your state) radio stations"
- "(your city), (your state) Internet"

Type in the city and/or state and a keyword in the web address search. That should bring up a variety of sites for newspapers, TV stations, radio stations, and Internet sites. Then click on the links to bring up detailed information about the media outlets. You also can call the media outlet directly for the information.

Step 2. Now it's time to gather the information from the media outlet's web sites. For newspapers and magazines, you have a couple of options: First, click on *"Business."* That will take you to the Business section of the paper. Look for the names of the business editor and business reporters. If you don't see them there, scroll to the bottom of the web page, you may see a *"Contact Us"* link. Click it. Typically that will take you to a comprehensive listing of all the newspaper contacts, or it will give you the names of the key business contacts.

Here are some examples of potential contacts from the different media outlets:

Newspapers

City editor

Business editor

Business reporters who cover the topic on which you want to be interviewed (ie., personal finance, investing, financial planning, etc.)

Magazines

Editor

Assistant editor

Writers who cover finance, economic news, etc.

Television, Radio, and Internet

News Director

Producer

Reporters who cover financial topics

Step 3. Some web sites are gold mines of information about potential contacts, while others may not be very helpful. That's when you'll need to call the station or publication yourself and ask for the information. When you call, you may have more success if you are as vague as possible with the receptionist. In other words, simply ask for the information, without a lengthy introduction or explanation. Many larger stations or publications are wary of giving out names and contact information over the phone. After all, those in the media often are contacted by dozens of people each day who want their 15 minutes of fame. But remember, you are offering a valuable service. If the receptionist does want more information, go ahead and say that you're a financial expert who'd like to help the station or publication increase its audience. Here's what to ask for: your contacts' names, phone numbers, fax numbers, and e-mail addresses.

Step 4. Another way to get contact information is to go to your local bookstore. Buy a copy of every local newspaper and financial magazine on the shelf, take them home, and pore through them to gain a list of the writers and editors who deal specifically with your topics. Don't limit yourself only to the financial sections, however. For example, on the inside front page of one of my local newspapers is a feature called "News 2 Use," which runs a page long and has all kinds of tips that the average consumer may find helpful, from gardening to health issues to budgeting and investing. I contacted the editor of that section and offered periodically to send him financial topics that I felt would be of interest to his readers. He now publishes the information I send to him every three to four weeks on different financial topics, such as "5 Ways to Save on Insurance" or "4 Ways You Can Save for Retirement." At the bottom, he lists my name and company name, so it's great free media exposure for me. This is an example of how it's important to be open to all sorts of opportunities in the media, not just the obvious ones.

THINK LIKE A REPORTER

To become the financial expert the media calls on, you must think like a reporter. You have to become a financial newshound. When you see an economic story or hear of a financial trend, you need to train your mind to determine whether it is a potential news opportunity for you. And if it is, you must know how to position yourself to be one of the financial experts who comments on it to the media. For example, when the government releases an economic report, you need to think about what that report means to the average person. Consider what it means to a retired person, to a working person, to a person putting kids through college. The first thing to do is to think of a way to personalize the news. Then use your expertise to translate the news from Wall Street to Main Street in a way that's easy to understand.

The key is to think about the media from all the different perspectives: the producer, the writer, and the viewer. Mentally envision yourself sitting in a helicopter flying above the news event, able to see every aspect of the story. From your perch in the sky, you can see all the different types of people in their fast-paced lives. And you're able to see how they would respond to this particular news event.

Key Questions Always to Ask Yourself

What does this issue mean to the viewers or readers?

Why would the producer or editor be interested in this story?

Why would the interviewer or writer be interested in this story?

Why would the viewer, listener, or reader be interested in this story?

If you can make a compelling case on a story idea and you feel that each of those people would benefit from the story angle you're proposing, then pitch the story to the media.

Let me give you an example of how to think like a reporter. It's very common for people to tune in to financial radio programs on Saturday and Sunday mornings. Knowing this, I went to my local television station, where I had been appearing regularly during the week, and suggested it do a financial segment as part of its Saturday programming. Typically, weekend mornings are slower news days, so the media are always looking for ways to fill time. The angle I used to sell the idea was that no other TV station had a financial expert on its news programs on the weekends. "Why not beat your competition to the punch," I told the producers, "by having me appear on the news program every Saturday morning?" I told them I'd do a weekly wrap-up on the stock market, talk about the upcoming week on Wall Street, answer a few viewer questions, and give a financial tip of the week. I developed a sample script. They liked the format, and now I am a regular part of their Saturday morning newscasts. Because of my idea, the station offers its viewers valuable financial information that no other local TV station was offering on Saturday morning. It positions this station as being responsive to the needs of its viewers, and it helps to further solidify my position as "the" financial expert for the TV station. It also allows me to be seen by a different audience from the one that sees me during the week, giving me even more exposure to potential clients.

MEDIA ACTION POINTS

✔ Learn to think like a news reporter.

✔ Think of story ideas that would appeal to the media and their audiences.

✔ Approach the media with new ideas so you can be interviewed more often.

✔ Observe the way competing media outlets present financial news, and create ways to do it better.

RATINGS PERIODS

Most media outlets are involved in what are called ratings periods or sweeps periods several times a year. During these times, media venues compete for the highest level of their respective audiences. Finishing with high marks not only gives the winners bragging rights that they are the "most watched" or "most listened to," but it also allows them to charge more for advertising, since most companies want to advertise on the station that has the largest listening or viewing audience.

Have you ever noticed that during some months of the year, all the episodes of your favorite programs are new? Or that the news stations start vigorously promoting what is coming up on their newscasts? Those are indications that the stations are in a ratings period. During ratings periods, news directors and producers are especially open to having guests who can help bump up their ratings and increase their viewing audience. These times offer you an opportunity to position yourself as the financial expert who can provide relevant and timely financial information to their audience and help them reach more people.

What are some ways that you can leverage the media during these ratings periods? Offer to appear on a regular basis. The first step to landing a regular appearance is to do a great job at your first interview. Be lively, come across as knowledgeable, and answer your questions in a way that gives the audience some memorable nuggets of information. As you're leaving the set, typically the producers will thank you for coming. In some cases they might say that you did a particularly nice job. If they say they were impressed with you, that's your chance to talk about coming back. If they appear lukewarm, ask:

- How do you feel the interview went?
- Was that what you were looking for?

The purpose of these questions is to get producers to open up to you about how they truly felt about your segment—good or bad. Producers won't sugarcoat things. Usually they'll tell you straight out how they thought your segment went. It's not always pleasant to hear bad news or an area that you could improve on. However, media outlets deal in reality, and they realize that there are countless potential guests on any given topic. If they discover that you're not the best one for them, they'll find someone else who can do the job the way they want it done. The key to both surviving and succeeding in the media is to clearly define what each media outlet wants and then deliver it. It's not about you doing what you consider to be your best work. Rather, it's all about you doing what the media outlet wants in the best way possible.

Here is what to say to your producers to begin appearing more frequently: "(Producer name), I have an idea to help your segment during sweeps. Research shows that people are more interested in money than ever before. They want someone who can take the news of Wall Street and explain it in an easy-to-understand way. Addressing that interest is a great way to help boost your ratings. Why don't you have me appear on a regular basis during the ratings period and let's see how it goes? We also could try having me answer viewer questions. Why don't we pick out some times and test it?"

The bottom line is that producers want to provide value for their audience. Everyone thinks about money—they do, their bosses do, and their viewers and listeners do. And they want to book financial guests on their shows who will come across well on the air and look like professionals. It's up to you to position yourself not only as a financial expert on the air, but also as an expert at obtaining feedback from your producers and then regularly setting your goals to exceed their expectations. In the media world, things change rapidly. If the media outlet sees its ratings begin to drop, it's executives will begin to evaluate carefully everything about their programming. They know on a daily basis exactly how they're stacking up to the competition. And they feel the pressure from their bosses to hit their goals.

PITCHING THE STORY

Once you know whom you're going to contact in the media, you need to develop a reason for the media to give you the time of day. Media outlets are looking for a way to put the news of the day in perspective for their audiences. The bad news is that unless you are proactive about contacting the media and can capture their attention, they are not going to call you out of the blue. The good news is that by assisting the media and offering them new and creative ways to think about and deliver the day's news, you can become one of their trusted sources.

In the media business, contacting the media with a story idea is referred to as "pitching a story." This is your way of letting them know about unique ways to report the news and to get them interested in using you as a source. Here's a simple rule to developing good story pitches: Approach the media with things you talk to your clients about.

If your clients are interested in a particular topic or investment product, then, most likely, the general public will have an interest too. If you can describe the issue well to your clients and you feel comfortable doing it, it's a natural transition to describe the issue to the media's audience.

There are five primary reasons to contact the media:

1. You received or gave out an award, were appointed to a committee, joined an organization, and so on.

2. You want to let the media know that you are available to comment on current news stories.

3. You want to inform the media about a news item.

4. You want to appear as a guest on a TV or radio program.

5. You would like to submit a guest financial article to be run in your local newspaper.

Whether you're a financial professional, stockbroker, insurance professional, or accountant, you'll be able to use these "story pitch" ideas to help you get into the media. I have divided this section of the chapter into three primary occupational classes. Each of these occupations will have different areas of expertise on which to comment to the media. For each occupation, I'll list the news angle you need to keep in mind and then specific story pitches that you can use when you contact the media.

CATEGORY 1: FINANCIAL ADVISORS AND STOCKBROKERS

News Angle Take the news from Wall Street and translate what it means to those on Main Street. It's your job to discuss the financial issues or products that are relevant today and describe them in a way that's easy to understand for the average investor.

"Pitch Story" Ideas

- "After the Federal Reserve meets today at (insert time), I will be available to discuss what their decisions mean to the average investor."

- "When (insert the name of a recognized company in your local area) releases its earnings numbers today, I will be available to provide expert commentary on what the news means to the average investor and the local economy."

- "Interest rates are at an all-time low. I'm available to inform your audience about their mortgage refinancing options and what to do with their monthly savings."

- "How much money do you really need to retire? This is the question that's plaguing your audience. I'm available to answer their questions and help them reach their retirement goals."

- "Is there more month left at the end of your money? I can discuss 'Five Ways to Put More Money in Your Pocket Today.' Call me right away."

- "Given the volatility in the stock market, I can provide your audience with tips on how to smooth out their portfolio."

- Release a report to the local media that shows the cost of going to the colleges in your area, with a note: "Your audience is concerned about how they can afford to send their children to college. I am available to discuss strategies your audience can use to save for their children's education."

Personal Marketing Angle   By speaking on a wide range of financial planning topics to the media audience, you are positioning yourself as a trusted financial expert who is knowledgeable about a wide variety of financial issues. You appeal to a large cross-section of potential clients.

CATEGORY 2: INSURANCE PROFESSIONALS

News Angle Consumers today have increased concerns about their safety, health and medical issues, and rising insurance costs. People have a heightened awareness of the importance of having the appropriate levels of different types of insurance, such as life, disability, long-term care, and medical.

"Pitch Story" Ideas

- "Whole life, variable universal life, or term insurance—the options can be so confusing. Your audience is interested in what types of insurance are best for them. I'll help them determine which types of insurance may be best for their situation."

- "How can you use life insurance to help fund retirement and education for your kids?"

- "How much insurance do you need?" (Give examples based on different incomes.) "I'll help your audience quickly calculate how much insurance they need without paying for insurance they don't need."

- Release a report that shows the average cost of a nursing home in your state. Then let the media know that you will explain those costs for viewers and describe the options available to help cover those expenses.

- "Worried about medical insurance after you retire? This is the question on the minds of many in your audience. I'll tell them what they need to consider before they retire."

- "Starting a small business is the dream of many Americans. However, before you open for business, here are (insert number) types of insurance coverage that no business owner should be without. Many in your audience are small business owners, and I can provide expert commentary on proper protection planning for entrepreneurs."

- "Now that you're retired, it's important for you to maintain your flexibility and independence. Here are five ways to help protect your and your family's financial independence as you grow older:

1. Purchase long-term care coverage.

2. Maintain appropriate levels of life, auto, home, and health insurance.

3. Evaluate the need for an umbrella liability policy to help protect you from lawsuits.

4. Make sure your estate planning is up-to-date.

5. Work closely with a qualified financial professional.

As a financial professional, I can provide expert commentary on financial issues that are important to your viewers. Call me today."

Personal Marketing Angle   You are building a reputation as an insurance professional who has experience in solving a variety of problems for your clients. You are helping dispel myths and falsehoods about insurance and positioning yourself as the expert on insurance options. You effectively state sample problems and then provide possible solutions through the various forms of insurance. When people think of insurance, they think of you.

CATEGORY 3: ACCOUNTANTS

News Angle   Offer tips and strategies on how the average viewer can take full advantage of the current tax laws, and educates on the pros and cons of potential new tax legislation.

"Pitch Story" Ideas

- "When the specifics of the new tax legislation are announced today, I will be available to provide some perspective as to what it means to your readers/viewers."

- "Would you like to cut your tax bill for next year? I am available to discuss five ways your audience can pay less to Uncle Sam. Call me today."

- "Last-minute tax planning strategies. I have three ways to help your viewers save on taxes even if they have procrastinated. Call on me today."

- "What are the most frequently overlooked tax deductions? As a tax expert, I can share with your audience some tax strategies in an easy-to-understand way. I look forward to hearing from you."

- "Here are four ways that small business owners can benefit from the new tax law." (Then select four strategies to discuss.)

- "Interested in saving money for your retirement and paying less in taxes? Here are three retirement plans that all small business owners should consider." (Then select four strategies to discuss.)

- "Considering pulling money out of your retirement accounts before 59½? Here's what you need to know to avoid the pitfalls of an early withdrawal."

Personal Marketing Angle   You have positioned yourself as a tax expert who can help clients pay less of their hard-earned money to Uncle Sam. You are very knowledgeable and up-to-date on the complex tax laws. You know how to help people in all kinds of situations, whether they own their own business, are about to retire, or just want to save on their tax bill so they'll have more money for their family.

Although most of the story pitch ideas just described can be used throughout the year with success, some story pitches are seasonal and will be most relevant and effective during particular times of the year (e.g., tax time, going back to school, saving for Christmas gifts, setting New Year's financial resolutions, etc.). Keep these seasonal events in mind as you're pitching your ideas. As you begin to see all news events as potential stories that you can "pitch" to the media, you'll begin to think of your own unique story angles.

MEDIA ACTION POINTS

15 Ways to Make News Today:

1. Announce an award that you've received.

2. Give recognition to a member of your staff.

3. Join an organization.

4. Announce the number of years you've had your business in town (i.e., 5, 10 years, etc.)

5. Present an award.

6. Tie into the local news.

7. Give a national story a local perspective.

8. Conduct a survey and release the results.

9. Comment on a news report, with the angle of "What does this mean to the average investor?"

10. Recognize a student of the month at the local high school.

11. Identify an issue that's important to your local community and offer to provide a "financial advisor" angle.

12. Send a press release to the local newspapers that you are now appearing as the financial expert on Channel X.

13. Speak at your local college or high school and have a picture taken and submitted to the paper.

14. Host a client appreciation event and have a photographer there from the newspaper's society page.

15. Speak on seasonal topics:

     ✔ Savings (December/January)

     ✔ Retirement (January)

     ✔ Taxes (April)

     ✔ Education (May)

COMMUNICATING WITH THE MEDIA

Let me share with you how I first got into the media. When I began my career as a financial professional, I quickly discovered that there were countless ways to go about marketing myself and my services. From conducting seminars to cold-calling on prospects to walking door to door in office buildings and industrial parks to meet business owners, I tried it all. And although I experienced some success with each of those options, I realized that each activity put me in front of only a limited audience. Unless I was doing a seminar, I was having to say the same thing over and over to each person I spoke with. Essentially, I was marketing myself on a one-to-one ratio. That wasn't the most effective use of my time.

As I drove around in my car, occasionally I listened to the radio. Throughout the day, a few news stations discussed business news, and someone would talk about what the stock market was doing. When I got home and flipped on the news, the anchors occasionally were interviewing a financial professional about what happened on Wall Street or regarding local business news. The more I listened and watched, I began to realize that this could be the marketing breakthrough I was searching for. I became convinced that appearing in the media might provide me with the opportunity to significantly boost my visibility and credibility. It could give me the opportunity to introduce myself to thousands of people instead of one at a time. I organized my media initiative. I researched the top media outlets that my target audience was tuned into and reading. Then I began sending each producer and editor at each of the media outlets I was targeting a fax that read:

Subject: Personal Finance Expert

When you need an expert to speak on complicated financial topics in an easy-to-understand and lively way, please call on me.

Thank you for your time.

Sincerely,

Derrick Kinney

I then handwrote, "P.S.—Thanks!" on the bottom of each fax.

I found the best time to send the faxes was late at night or very early in the morning. That way the recipients would receive the fax when they first got into the office, before they had to start "putting out fires" in the newsroom. Faxes received in the middle of the day often are put aside for the pressing news of the day, and they become missed opportunities. I sent my faxes consistently every two weeks, and after about two months, a call came in from a television producer. I was asked to appear on an afternoon television program.

VISUALIZE THE SUCCESSFUL INTERVIEW

Once my first TV interview was scheduled, I practiced and prepared myself to make the most of the opportunity. I sat in front of the bathroom mirror every night rehearsing my answers to possible questions. I sat on the couch in my living room and practiced speaking confidently with the host. Before I went on the TV set to do the interview, I visualized everything in my mind. I saw myself arriving at the studio. I pictured myself meeting my producer with a big smile and firm handshake. Then I envisioned my interview going so smoothly that at the end of it, the host would say, "Wow, we need to have you on more often. You really described things in a way that people can understand. That was great!" And here's the good news: Just as I hoped, the interview went well and the producer came to me afterward and said that I was "made for television" and that she would like me to be a regular guest on the program.

What's the moral of this story? I created a plan, executed the plan, and then carefully prepared for my opportunity. When the opportunity came, I visualized myself succeeding. Then in the actual interview, I put my best foot forward and achieved positive results. But most important, I identified my strength and then exploited my strength by appearing on television. I want you to identify your unique strength and then focus on using it to get into the media. Remember that every day media outlets search for knowledgeable and trustworthy financial professionals to inform and educate their audiences. By following these steps, *you* can become the expert the media calls on—so read on!

HOW TO TALK TO THE MEDIA

Now that you have a story to pitch to the media, it's time to communicate your message in a way that makes them take notice and act on it. There are four main ways to communicate with the media: fax, e-mail, by phone, or in person. Each method of communication will appeal to different people in the media and will get the attention of editors and producers at different times.

The best system that I've found is first to send faxes or e-mails to your media contacts. Then consider following up with a phone call. After all, people in the media receive countless unwanted phone calls every day. If you call them, you run the risk that they'll associate you with all the other people calling them and trying to act friendly in order to get something. Interestingly, of all the interviews I have done over the years, none of them happened as a result of me calling a media contact on the phone or meeting her in person. A common misconception regarding the local media is that you have to know a reporter or news anchor personally to be interviewed. That could not be further from the truth. The key is to contact the media in a way that makes you stand out and uniquely positions you as a financial expert who can deliver information to their audience in an easy-to-understand way. In short, faxes and e-mails are powerful tools, and they capture the attention of the media better than phone calls.

TRACK YOUR
MEDIA CONTACTS

Think back to earlier in the chapter, where I discussed how to identify the various media outlets in your area. Each of those media outlets will have different people who handle different aspects of the news. For example, most newspapers have a weekly section titled something like "People on the Move" or "Business Promotions/Announcements". Typically this section shows a person's picture and one sentence on their recent promotion, appointment to a board, or other accomplishment. If you want to have your name, company name, and picture mentioned in that section of the paper, you must find out who coordinates that section and send him or her the information to be printed. It's a quick, easy, and effective way to begin getting your name in front of people. It's also a good way to "get your feet wet" and practice sending things to be published by the media.

The best way to keep track of your media contacts is to create a simple Media Contacts spreadsheet that you keep in a file. On the spreadsheet, list your contacts' names, titles, media outlets, phone and fax numbers, and e-mail addresses. You also can list different categories based on what types of press releases or stories each contact would be interested in receiving. Table 2.2 provides a sample.

This spreadsheet will become your road map to the local media. Treat it as if it's made of pure gold. The people listed are the very ones you will be contacting on a regular basis to send story ideas and press releases to. Maintaining this document is absolutely critical to your success in the media. It's also vital that you update your spreadsheet on a regular basis. In the media business, it is very common for people to take on different assignments or move to a different media outlet. For example, the reporter who interviewed you last week could be transferred to another part of the newspaper at any time. Or she may jump ship and go to a competitor. If your contact moves to a different media outlet that is still in your local area, it's important for you to stay in touch so that you can continue to be one of her news sources. Also, it gives you the opportunity of being interviewed in an additional media outlet, which means more free publicity for you in front of a potentially new audience. By keeping this list continually updated, you'll ensure that your press releases are sent to the right person.

MEDIA ACTION POINTS

✔ Keep your Media Contacts spreadsheet updated at all times.

✔ Stay in touch with your contacts so they will stay in touch with you.

✔ Know what is happening at your local media outlets.

Table 2.2 Media Contacts

Newspapers

Contact Name	Paper	Title	Phone Number	Fax Number	E-mail Address	General	Columns	Awards
Bob Smith	Main Street Newspaper	Editor	555-555-1111	555-555-1112	bsmith@mainstnews.com	X	X	
Susan Jones	Main Street Newspaper	Reporter	555-555-1122	555-555-1112	sjones@mainstnews.com			X

Magazine Contacts

Contact Name	Magazine	Title	Phone Number	Fax Number	E-mail Address	General	Columns	Awards
Jill Rogers	Main Street Magazine	Editor	555-555-2222	555-555-2223	jrogers@mainstmag.com	X	X	
Jane Smith	Main Street Magazine	Writer	555-555-2222	555-555-2223	jsmith@mainstmag.com	X		X

Television Contacts

Contact Name	Television Station	Title	Phone Number	Fax Number	E-mail Address	General	Columns	Awards
Bob Watson	Producer	Channel 7 News	555-555-3333	555-555-3334	bwatson@channel7.com	X		
Ed Johnson	Producer	Channel 9 News	555-555-4444	555-555-4445	ejohnson@channel9.com	X		

Radio Contacts

Contact Name	Radio Station	Title	Phone Number	Fax Number	E-mail Address	General	Columns	Awards
Joe Williams	KAAA	News Director	555-555-5555	555-555-5556	jwilliams@kaaa.com	X		

Internet Contacts

Contact Name	Web Site	Title	Phone Number	Fax Number	E-mail Address	General	Columns	Awards
Lauren Gray	Abcfinancialnews.com	Reporter	555-555-6666	555-555-6667	Lauren@abcfinancial.com	X		

THE PRESS RELEASE

The press release is how you will communicate most often with the media. Press releases can be faxed, e-mailed, or mailed to news contacts. The purpose of press releases is to let the media know about a specific news item or story you can help them with.

Study this sample template as you create your press releases.

FOR IMMEDIATE RELEASE (Bold, 16-point font)

CONTACT: (Your name or your assistant's name)
                (Your phone number)

(Title of Press Release: always bold and centered)

(City, State)-(Date)-(Your name), xxxx xxxxxx xxxxxxx xxxx (City) xxxxx xxxxx (Company name), xxxx xxxxx x xxx xxxx xxxx (Organization name).

xxx (Organization name) xx (Give two- to three-sentence description of what the organization does).

-##-
(dash, number sign, number sign, dash centered—
this is the proper press release ending)

Please use picture on file.

ACTIVE VS. PASSIVE MEDIA RELATIONS

There are two primary types of media relations: active and passive. "Active media relations" means that you are being interviewed by the newspaper, a magazine, or a TV or radio station. In active media relations, you are actively involved in the media. Passive media relations includes getting your name, company name, and picture in the newspaper, trade journals or magazines, with little work required on your part. You simply send in the information to the media, and they publish it for free. To get the biggest bang for your buck, it is critical for you to focus on both active and passive media relations, in order for prospective clients to begin to notice you.

Active media exposure includes:

- Being interviewed by a newspaper or magazine reporter
- Being interviewed by a television or radio station
- Being interviewed by a financial Internet site
- Having a feature story written about you
- Having a guest financial column printed
- Doing a "Money Makeover" for a person, with a newspaper or magazine reporter writing a special feature article on how you work as a financial professional

ACTIVE MEDIA ACTIONS

This system is simple. Just edit the fax or e-mail the following templates with all the correct information to *all* your media contacts. The purpose of this fax is to let them know that you are a financial expert they can contact to be a source for their news stories.

Sample Fax Template for
Newspapers, Magazines, and the Internet

FAX—Please Hand Deliver   **(Insert Your Company Logo Here)**

CONFIDENTIAL

Date: (Date)

To: (Contact name)
              (Station or Publication name)
Phone: (Phone number of contact)
Fax: (Fax number of contact)

From: **(Your Name)**
                   (Your Company)
Phone: **(Your Phone Number with Extension)**
Fax: **(Your Fax Number)**

Pages: **1**
Subject: **Expert Commentary for Your Personal Finance Stories**

Dear (insert their first name):

Please keep my name on file for upcoming personal finance stories that you need expert commentary on. I am able to take complex financial issues and make them easy to understand for your readers.

Sample topics I could discuss include:
   * 3 Steps to Consistent Returns in Inconsistent Times
   * 5 Tips to Retiring Early
   * 5 Strategies for Retirees to Boost their Fixed Income
   * How to Jump Start Your Tax Planning for (insert year)
   * 4 Tips to Protecting your Retirement Plan
   * Layoffs Ahead: 3 Survival Tips
   * 4 Steps to a Successful Career Transition
   * 5 Ways to Keep More Money in Your Pocket Today

Call me at: Office: (your office number)
                 Cell: (your cell number)
                 Home: (your home number)

I return calls quickly. I hope to hear from you soon!

Thank you for your time,

(Sign your name)
(Your Name)
(Your Title)

Handwrite, *"P.S.—Thanks!"*

Sample E-mail Template for
Newspapers, Magazines, and the Internet

To: **(Contact)**
CC:
Subject: **Expert Commentary for Your Personal Finance Stories**

Dear (insert their first name):

Please keep my name on file for upcoming personal finance stories that you need expert commentary on. I am able to take complex financial issues and make them easy to understand for your readers.

Sample topics I could discuss include:
 * 3 Steps to Consistent Returns in Inconsistent Times
 * 5 Tips to Retiring Early
 * 5 Strategies for Retirees to Boost their Fixed Income
 * How to Jump Start Your Tax Planning for (insert year)
 * 4 Tips to Protecting your Retirement Plan
 * Layoffs Ahead: 3 Survival Tips
 * 4 Steps to a Successful Career Transition
 * 5 Ways to Keep More Money in Your Pocket Today

I return calls quickly.

Thank you for your time,

(Your Name)
(Your Title)
Office: (your office number)
Cell: (your cell number)
Home: (your home number)

P.S.—Thanks!

Sample Fax Template for Television and Radio

FAX—Please Hand Deliver   (Insert Your Company Logo Here)

CONFIDENTIAL

Date: (Date)

To: (Contact name)
               (Station or Publication name)
Phone: (Phone number of contact)
Fax: (Fax number of contact)

From: (Your Name)
               (Your Company)
Phone: (Your Phone Number with Extension)
Fax: (Your Fax Number)

Pages: 1

Subject: Expert Commentary for Your Personal Finance Stories

Dear (insert their first name):

Your (viewers or listeners) have an unquenchable thirst for timely financial information. I can help put today's issues in perspective for your audience.

I can complement your existing "experts" by not being too analytical. Instead, I talk in a (viewer or listener)-friendly and easy-to-understand way. I specialize in personal finance issues.

Sample topics I could discuss include:
    * 3 Steps to Consistent Returns in Inconsistent Times
    * 5 Tips to Retiring Early
    * 5 Strategies for Retirees to Boost their Fixed Income
    * Jump Start Your Tax Planning for (insert year)
    * 4 Tips to Protecting your Retirement Plan
    * Layoffs Ahead: 3 Survival Tips
    * 4 Steps to a Successful Career Transition
    * 5 Ways to Keep More Money in Your Pocket Today

Call me at: Office: (your office number)
                 Cell: (your cell number)
                 Home: (your home number)

I return calls quickly. I hope to hear from you soon!

Thank you for your time,

(Sign your name)
(Your Name)
(Your Title)

P.S.—Thanks!

Sample E-mail Template for Television and Radio

To: **(Contact)**
CC:
Subject: **Expert Commentary for Your Personal Finance Stories**

Dear (insert their first name):

Your (viewers or listeners) have an unquenchable thirst for timely financial infor-mation. I can help put today's issues in perspective for your audience.

I can complement your existing "experts" by not being too analytical. Instead, I talk in a (viewer or listener)-friendly and easy-to-understand way. I specialize in personal finance issues.

Sample topics I could discuss include:
    * 3 Steps to Consistent Returns in Inconsistent Times
    * 5 Tips to Retiring Early
    * 5 Strategies for Retirees to Boost their Fixed Income
    * How to Jump Start Your Tax Planning for (insert year)
    * 4 Tips to Protecting your Retirement Plan
    * Layoffs Ahead: 3 Survival Tips
    * 4 Steps to a Successful Career Transition
    * 5 Ways to Keep More Money in Your Pocket Today

I return calls quickly.

Thank you for your time,

(Your Name)
(Your Title)

Office: (your office number)
Cell: (your cell number)
Home: (your home number)

P.S.—Thanks!

TAP INTO TODAY'S NEWS

Use the templates to let the media know you are available to comment on financial news stories taking place today, such as Federal Reserve meetings, local company announcing earnings, and release of a key economic report.

The following templates are a great way for you to target newspapers to be quoted as a financial expert. This approach works best using e-mail, since it is more immediate.

Sample Fax Template for Newspapers

FAX – Please Hand Deliver   **(Insert Your Company Logo Here)**

CONFIDENTIAL

Date: **(Date)**

To: **(Producer name)**
                 (Publication name)
Phone: **(Phone number of contact)**
Fax: **(Fax number of contact)**

From: **(Your Name)**
               (Your Company)
Phone: **(Your Phone Number with Extension)**
Fax: **(Your Fax Number)**

Pages: **1**

Subject: **(INSERT SUBJECT-EXAMPLE:**
               FEDERAL RESERVE ANNOUNCEMENT)

Dear (insert their first name):

If you need a financial expert to comment on what today's Federal Reserve meeting may mean to the average investor, please call me.

I can be reached at: Office: (your office number)
                         Cell: (your cell number)
                         Home: (your home number)

I return calls quickly. I hope to hear from you soon!
Thank you for your time,
(Sign your name)

(Your Name)
(Your Title)

P.S.—Thanks!

Sample E-mail Template for Newspapers

To: **(Contact)**
CC:
Subject: **(INSERT SUBJECT-EXAMPLE: FEDERAL RESERVE ANNOUNCE-**
              MENT TODAY)

Dear (insert their first name):

If you need a financial expert to comment on what today's Federal Reserve meeting may mean to the average investor, please call me.

I can be reached at: Office: (your office number)
                              Cell: (your cell number)
                              Home: (your home number)

I return calls quickly. I hope to hear from you soon!

Thank you for your time,

(Your Name)
(Your Title)

P.S.—Thanks!

HAVING THE MEDIA WRITE AN ARTICLE ABOUT YOU

One of the best ways really to stand out in your local buying area is to have the media focus its attention solely on you, by writing a feature article on something noteworthy you or your company has done. For example, your local newspaper could publish a story about:

- A profile on your community service work
- Your leadership in an organization that you are heavily involved with
- A new program or business initiative you have started
- A book you've written
- How you recognize the top students at the area schools
- How you've launched a new web site
- A new product or service you are offering

The key to remember is that the media needs content to fill up the pages of its newspapers and magazines. Most newspapers have a "Local" section that runs daily or a few days per week. This is the best place to target for an article like this. If you're not letting the media know about something newsworthy that you or your company is doing, you're missing out on a great opportunity to help promote yourself to more of your ideal prospects. While this approach has a higher success rate with newspapers, you also can approach local television stations with the story idea. Emphasize that you're a local person who is doing something to help the community. The media really like stories about local "unsung heroes."

Here are a few sample press release templates for you to use as a guide. Just insert your information into the body of the fax cover sheet template and fax it to the appropriate media contact. You also can use the e-mail template.

Sample Community Service Press Release

FOR IMMEDIATE RELEASE—Possible Feature Story for Local Section

CONTACT: (Your name or your assistant's name)
                      (Your phone number)

Local Businessman Enjoys Recognizing Top Students

(City, State)-(Date) - (Your name), a (your title) with the (city) office of (company name) enjoys giving back to the community. Having built a successful financial planning business, (your last name) recognizes the need for more business leaders to encourage students to succeed. Every month (your last name) goes to Good Student High School and presents the (your name) Top Student Award. The student is nominated by his or her teachers, and the award recognizes outstanding student leadership inside and outside the classroom. The student receives a certificate and a check for $50.

"It's important to recognize student leaders," said (your last name). "By encouraging them now, we're fostering tomorrow's community leaders." (Your last name) is also an active member of (insert an organization name) and appears on/in (insert media name) as a financial expert.

-##-

Photo opportunity: (Your name) presenting the award to next month's student recipient at Good Student High School.

Sample Business History Press Release

FOR IMMEDIATE RELEASE—Possible Feature Story for Local Section

CONTACT: (Your name or your assistant's name)
             (Your phone number)

Three Generations Trust (insert your name)
with Their Financial Planning

(City, State)-(Date)-One way (your full name), a (title) with (company name), builds his financial planning practice is on recommendations from satisfied clients. He just didn't expect them to all come from the same family.

Client Virginia Smith of Smithville, 83, recently called (your last name)'s office to express her excitement that three generations of her family were working with (your full name) and applying his investment counsel.

Helen's son, Tom Smith, was the first to begin working with (your last name). Soon to follow was Tom's son, Joe Smith, who quickly saw the benefits of a financial advisor and began his financial planning. After seeing the success Tom and his son, Joe, were having with their investments and (your last name)'s advice, Tom referred his mother, Virginia Smith.

"It is an incredible feeling to know our practice has such a positive impact on this family and so many others," (your last name) said. "A heritage of prudent money management is as important as the values and traditions that are passed down through a family."

(Your last name) recently celebrated (insert number of years) of being in business and will be holding a Community Open House to thank his clients and their guests for his success. If you would like to attend, please call: (your phone number).

-##-

Possible contacts to be interviewed for this story:
Virginia Smith (555-555-5555), Tom Smith (777-777-7777)

Sample New Resource Press Release

FOR IMMEDIATE RELEASE

CONTACT: **(Your name or your assistant's name)**
                  (Your phone number)

Local Advisor Launches Informational Web Site

(City, State)-(Date) - (Your name), of the (city) office of (company name), has launched a new web site (insert web site address). The informational site has links to all types of financial news, specific (your company name) accounts and an opportunity to sign up for (your name's) free financial e-mail newsletter.

The web site offers various financial planning tools, including a retirement calculator, education planner, and cash flow and asset allocation tools. The site also offers up-to-the-minute stock market quotes.

"The web site is intended to be a financial resource for local residents," said (your last name).

-##-

Sample New Product Press Release

FOR IMMEDIATE RELEASE

CONTACT: (Your name or your assistant's name)
                 (Your phone number)

Local Advisor Offers New Investment Product

(City, State)-(Date) - (Your company name), in conjunction with (investment company name), is offering a new (name of investment product).

What makes this product unique is:

- (Insert bullet point 1)
- (Insert bullet point 2)
- (Insert bullet point 3)

For more information, (your name) can be reached at (your phone number). His offices are located in (city).

-##-

DO A MONEY MAKEOVER

Contact your local media outlets and offer to do a "Money Makeover" for a selected member of their audience. Here's how it works: You do a complete financial analysis for a selected person, and the media interviews you and the person for a feature story. This can be a great way to demonstrate the quality of work you do, and it provides a valuable service to the media's audience. Here are some sample templates to start a money makeover.

Sample Fax Money Makeover Template for Newspapers, Television, and the Internet

FAX—Please Hand Deliver   **(Insert Your Company Logo Here)**

CONFIDENTIAL

Date: **(Date)**

To: **(Contact name)**
                 (Station or Publication name)
Phone: **(Phone number of contact)**
Fax: **(Fax number of contact)**

From: **(Your Name)**
               (Your Company)
Phone: **(Your Phone Number with Extension)**
Fax: **(Your Fax Number)**

Pages: **1**

Subject: **MONEY MAKEOVER Feature Story Idea**

Dear (insert their first name):

As a local financial advisor in (insert area), I wanted to let you know I am available to do a "Money Makeover" for a selected member of your audience. I will provide a complete financial analysis for the person you select, and you can do a special feature story and show the "Before" and "After." Please call to discuss the details.

I can be reached at: Office: (your office number)
                           Cell: (your cell number)
                           Home (your home number)

I return calls quickly. I hope to hear from you soon!

Thank you for your time,
(Sign your name)

(Your Name)
(Your Title)

P.S.—Thanks!

Sample E-mail Money Makeover Template

To: **(Contact)**
CC:
Subject: **MONEY MAKEOVER Feature Story Idea**

Dear (insert their first name):

As a local financial advisor in (insert area), I wanted to let you know I am available to do a "Money Makeover" for a selected member of your audience. I will provide a complete financial analysis for the person you select, and you can do a special feature story and show the "Before" and "After." Please call to discuss the details.

I can be reached at: Office: (your office number)
                              Cell: (your cell number)
                              Home (your home number)

I return calls quickly. I hope to hear from you soon!

Thank you for your time,

(Your Name)
(Your Title)

P.S.—Thanks!

PASSIVE MEDIA

In passive media, the media outlets do the work for you. Examples of passive media include:

- Getting your name, company name, and picture printed as a "Business Person/Executive on the Move"
- Having a new employee's name, your company name, and the employee's picture printed
- Getting your picture in the paper as you're presenting an award
- Having your name, company name, and picture printed as having been named to serve on a board, committee, or other position of power and privilege

PASSIVE MEDIA ACTIONS

Another way to leverage your local newspapers, magazines, and business publications is by sending press releases to the media—you'll receive free publicity with little or no work on your part! The system is simple, but slightly different from active media press releases. These press releases are best sent by mail.

Here are four simple steps to getting your name and picture in the newspaper through passive media relations:

1. Edit the press release template.
2. Print the press release on your letterhead.
3. Hand-address a legal-size envelope.
4. Put the press release and photograph into the envelope and mail.

Following this strategy will virtually guarantee that your information and picture will be printed in the newspaper. Here are some sample press releases.

Sample Award Recipient Press Release

Please print the following award announcement and enclosed picture.

FOR IMMEDIATE RELEASE

CONTACT: (Your name or your assistant's name)
             (Your phone number)

Local Advisor (Receives Honor, Named to X Committee, Awarded, etc.)

(City, State)-(Date) - (Your name), a (your title) with (your company), was recently honored with the (name of award). (Include a sentence about the award and why you received it.)

-##-

Please use the enclosed picture.

Sample New Hire Press Release

Please print the following announcement and enclosed picture.

FOR IMMEDIATE RELEASE

CONTACT: (Your name or your assistant's name)
              (Your phone number)

Local Financial Advisor Hires New Employee

(City, State)-(Date) - (New employee name) has joined the (city) financial planning office of (your name) of (company name), as a (title).

-##-

Please use the enclosed picture.

Sample Honorary Title Press Release

Please print the following announcement and enclosed picture.

FOR IMMEDIATE RELEASE

CONTACT: (Your name or your assistant's name)
              (Your phone number)

(Your name) Honored as (Name of Title)

(City, State)-(Date) - (Your name), a (your title) with the (city) office of (company name), has been appointed a member of the company's prestigious (name of special group).

-##-

Please use picture on file.

Sample New Member Press Release

Please print the following announcement and enclosed picture.

FOR IMMEDIATE RELEASE

CONTACT: (Your name or your assistant's name)
                        (Your phone number)

(Your Name) Named a Member of (Organization Name)

(City, State)-(Date) - (Your name), a (insert your title) with the (city) office of (company name), has been named a member of the (organization name).
The (organization name) is (give a two- to three-sentence description of what the organization does).

-##-

Please use picture on file.

Sample Professional Designation Press Release

Please print the following announcement and enclosed picture.

FOR IMMEDIATE RELEASE

CONTACT: (Your name or your assistant's name)
                        (Your phone number)

(Your Name) Earns (Name of Designation) Designation

(City, State)-(Date) - (Your name), a (insert your title) with (company name), has earned the (insert professional designation name) designation from (insert college name). (Write two to three sentences as to what the professional designation focuses on.)

-##-

Please use picture on file.

KNOW THE GROUND RULES

As you begin to implement this system, keep in mind that the media people you'll be targeting are busy. It is important for you to repeat this process frequently until they take notice of you and you get your first interview opportunity. Your break may come the first month (depending on the needs of the media), or it may take several months. The time frame can vary depending on the number of media outlets in your local area and the size of your local audience. The key is to stay consistent and try to tailor your message to best appeal to the media outlet you're targeting.

When you send e-mails, there are a couple of rules to remember. If you have multiple contacts and you're not sure who will be interested in your pitch, a blanket message is the easiest way to go. Just type in the addresses in the "bcc" (blind carbon copies) box, and send out the message without a specific greeting. This way you are respecting the privacy of your recipients, and you are not revealing the fact that you're sending a message out to dozens of people. Each recipient will believe that he or she is the lucky one to get your message. However, if you've worked with a particular reporter or writer in the past or you have a good relationship with a contact, you may want to send a specific message that is personalized for that individual. He or she may appreciate hearing from you in a more personal e-mail. You'll most likely get better results this way.

To succeed in the media, it's important to tailor your message to the different media outlets that you're targeting. It's also important to understand the schedule of each media outlet. Some producers, writers, and editors operate on a daily basis; therefore, they have news and interview needs that change on a daily basis. Other media contacts may write stories that appear weekly, biweekly, or monthly. Those individuals, who have more time to work on a story, may want a more in-depth viewpoint. Find out what your contacts' needs are and then offer something of value to fill those needs. Imagine how much information media outlets are inundated with each day. Because of that you'll need to plan on contacting your desired media outlets multiple times before your name will begin to stand out to them.

I can't stress enough the importance of closely following your fixed calendar. Continue to focus the majority of your time on generating sales today—not just so you can grow your business, but so that you *stay* in business. The media is exciting, and you may be tempted to devote most of your time to securing your first appearance. However, you need to rein in some of that energy and focus your media work to just one to two hours per week at first. That will allow you to spend quality time on growing your business and earning a paycheck, while you plant the seeds for media success.

MEDIA ACTION POINTS

✔ Be consistent as you implement this system.

✔ Plan on contacting the media outlets multiple times before they'll begin to recognize you.

✔ Follow your fixed calendar and do weekly media work.

✔ Stay focused on seeing clients and generating a paycheck.

✔ Continue your existing marketing efforts and let your media exposure complement it.

MEDIA MADE SIMPLE

As you begin sending press releases and items to the media, it's important to space them out properly. It's better to have your name and picture in the paper once a month instead of four times in one week and then not at all for four months. The goal is to create the appearance that you are in the media all the time. By spacing out what you send to the media, you can accomplish that. Use a spreadsheet like the one in Table 2.3 to keep track of what you send to the media to be published.

Let's be honest—time is money. As a financial professional, your time is best spent either in front of clients making money or directly marketing yourself and your business through the media. As I mentioned, while you can certainly implement this program yourself, I recommend that, if possible, you have your staff work through the program with you. Have them do the research and begin contacting the media on your behalf. Let them print and send the faxes and type up and send the e-mails. Remember these

Table 2.3 Media Resources

DATE: _____

		What Was Sent / Date Sent																	
Newspapers	Contact Name																		
Television Stations	Contact Name																		
Radio Stations	Contact Name																		
Local Magazines/ Publications	Contact Name																		
Internet Sites	Contact Name																		

key questions to ask yourself when submitting a press release: Will this particular media outlet's audience find this information of interest? And if so, why? If you answer those two questions before you write your press release, you will greatly increase the odds of the media interviewing you about it or printing it. Then when the media calls on you, you'll be the one in the spotlight doing the interviews. Talk to your staff about this program and how important it is. Let them know that when members of the media call for you, they are to receive preferential treatment. If you're in a meeting, have them take a message. Make sure they let the media know that you will return their calls right away. If possible, have your staff interrupt what you're doing so you can speak with any reporter who calls you.

Remember, when opportunity knocks, you want to be the first one to open the door. Sometimes the person who gets quoted for a news story is simply the first financial professional a reporter could get in touch with. Make sure that person is you!

THE MEDIA QUICK-START PLAN

Now it's time to hit the ground running by implementing the 10-Day Media Quick-Start Plan. Think of this as an all-out media blitz.

Here's an overview of the five key steps to get started:

1. *Discover* who your ideal clients are.
2. *Identify* which media outlets you may be best suited for.
3. *Research* your local media outlets and complete the Media Contacts spreadsheet.
4. *Fax* all the media outlets the Introductory Fax to let them know that you are available to comment as a financial expert.
5. *Fax* or e-mail the media that same day when breaking news events or economic events occur so you can comment on them.

MEDIA ACTION POINTS

Implement this 10-day action plan to jump-start your media campaign.

Day 1: Discover who your ideal clients are.

Day 2: Identify which media outlets you may be best suited for based on your strengths.

Day 3: Research your local media outlets.

Day 4: Research your local media outlets and collect contact names and information.

Day 5: Identify which media outlets you want to target.

Day 6: Send introductory faxes to your media outlets. (*Frequency: Repeat this step every two to four weeks.*)

Day 7: Send e-mails to newspapers about breaking financial news stories (i.e., Fed meeting, local economic report about to be released, etc.). Send two to four hours before the news event is scheduled to occur. (*Frequency: Repeat this step every two to four weeks.*)

Day 8: Have some color 4 × 6 pictures taken of you. Edit the press release announcing an award you received or something you have done. Then mail your press release and your picture to the "Workfaces/Executives on the Move/People" section of the newspaper. (*Frequency: Repeat this step every four weeks.*)

Day 9: Contact your local newspapers and specialized business newspapers about submitting a guest financial column that would be of great interest to their readers. Tell them you'd like to know if they could run your article on a "space available" basis.

Day 10: Fill in your Media Contacts Tracker spreadsheet to monitor your progress.

IT'S TIME FOR YOU TO BREAK IN

You're going to do a lot of work before you actually appear in the media for the first time. But keep in mind that you're working so hard because of the exponential exposure that the media offers. One interview in the paper or an interview on TV or the radio may be seen or heard by thousands of potential clients or customers for you and your business.

To be truly successful in the media and to establish a presence where people recognize you and remember you, it takes multiple appearances on a frequent basis. Appearing in the media once allows you to say that you've done it, but it certainly doesn't allow you to maximize your exposure. As I discussed in Chapter One, it takes a while for your audience to begin to recognize and accept you as "their" financial expert.

Media outlet needs you. And to reach the types of clients you want to work with, you need them too. The media's primary job is to report the news in a way that makes the most sense to their readers or viewers. What do those readers and viewers want? They want the news, not advertisements. Of course, once you are in the media and have established a rapport with your contacts by providing a service to their audience, you *will* be advertising yourself, but in a subtle way. And that's the beauty of media relations. You gain massive exposure for you and your company without having to pay the high advertising rates.

CHALLENGE

There are 365 days of media opportunities throughout the year. And on each of those days, media outlets are looking to bring the best news product possible to their viewers. There is no reason that you shouldn't be in the media. As you prepare your material and send it out, begin visualizing yourself as the expert who should appear before an audience. Consistently follow the Media Quick-Start Plan, and you're off to the races. Implement these strategies and over time you'll begin to experience the tremendous benefits that media exposure offers.

CHAPTER THREE

LEARN
THE ROPES

Congratulations! You've gotten your big break and you have your first interview scheduled. The time you've spent implementing your media campaign is starting to open doors for you. Now it's time to do your prep work so you give the best interview possible and are invited back again and again. Getting your foot in the door is only the first step. In order to have a winning strategy with the media, you must create a plan for your first interview and then implement that plan to achieve the success you envision. In this chapter I'll discuss ways for you to do exactly that. You'll learn how to play a critical role in how the media outlets prepare for your interviews. You'll also learn the tricks of the trade so that you can make things easy for your media contacts and communicate exactly the message you want to thousands of ideal prospects at one time.

OPPORTUNITY KNOCKS

When a reporter or producer calls you to do an interview, he or she typically will have a topic in mind for you to discuss. You may be asked to comment on a breaking financial news story and what it means to the local community or to help educate the audience on a financial topic or issue that is of particular interest. The key is to find out before the interview what you're going to be speaking on so that you can prepare by practicing your answers and mentally visualizing the interview ahead of time.

As I have discussed, discipline yourself to accept only those interview opportunities that are a clear fit for your area of expertise. If you feel the topic or the questions you may be asked fall outside of your specialty, don't hesitate to refer the opportunity to a more qualified person. By doing so, you'll come out looking like a hero by connecting the media to the right person. Your media contact will remember your help and will call on you again because she knows that either you can do the interview or you will refer the opportunity to another colleague. When you give a colleague an opportunity in the media because he is better qualified to speak on a topic, you're also building up a few favors with him that you may need down the road. In either case, you have helped solve the reporter's problem. The more problems you help media contacts solve, the more future opportunities you'll have.

Now you know what your interview topic is, and you've agreed to speak on it. How can you best prepare yourself for your interview? Here are three easy steps to get prepared:

MEDIA ACTION POINTS

1. Identify the main points you would like to convey concerning your selected topic.

2. Practice asking and answering sample questions on the topic. As you listen to your answers, keep repeating the phrases you like until you can say them without thinking, and disregard phrases that may come across as too technical for your audience.

3. Deliver the interview just as you practiced it. Calmly and coolly answer the questions in a way that makes sense to the audience.

COACHING THE MEDIA

With all the news covered 24/7, reporters can't possibly be knowledgeable about everything. Instead, they rely on the experts they call on for interviews to give them guidance and information. That creates a big opportunity for financial professionals, like you, to be one of the experts called on to be interviewed for financial news stories.

The media report on two primary types of news:

1. *"Straightforward" news items.* These include events that are easily understood. For these events, it is not necessary to interview an expert who can explain the event in detail. Examples of these news items include traffic accidents, a grand opening of a new downtown building, or a local celebrity who was honored with an award.

2. *"Explanation" news items.* These include media stories about topics that require more in-depth coverage. Often experts who can help the audience better understand the information are interviewed. Examples of this type of news include a consumer confidence survey that was just released, a research study showing that most Americans aren't saving enough money for retirement, or a news story that uncovers corporate fraud and how it will impact the economy and local investors.

"Explanation" news items represent your best opportunities to be interviewed. When a news item like this occurs, media outlets want to keep their viewers and listeners informed. Since these stories require further explanation, typically the media will invite a financial expert to explain the news item and discuss what it means to the average investor.

Here are some sure-fire strategies to position yourself as the expert the media calls on for "explanation" news events:

- When breaking financial stories occur, let the media know that you are available to provide expert commentary for their news stories.

- Because the television and radio news programs can broadcast 24 hours a day, they will report business news before newspapers can. First try to reach your TV or radio media contacts. If you can't reach them, then try the newspaper contacts, since they won't report the story until the next morning.

- Let local media outlets know in advance that when breaking financial news occurs and they need an expert who is a skilled communicator, they can call on you. Tell them that you return calls quickly and can be reached day or night.

EARNING THE MEDIA'S TRUST

As you begin to work more closely with the media, your role is to help them determine the key points their audience needs to know about a given topic or issue. For example, if the media are doing a story on the unemployment rate in the local area, they'll announce that unemployment increased by 2 percent. If they stop there, they're merely stating a fact, and their reporting is one-dimensional. But their reporting is at its best when the media can delve into the topic more deeply and illustrate what it means in the lives of their audience. In our example, the media could provide more in-depth coverage by bringing in an expert like you to answer the question "What does the rising unemployment rate in our area mean to the average person?" The media are looking for ways to take a bland statistic and make it mean something to their audiences.

You might comment that a rising unemployment rate can have a negative effect on the local economy or that people may have to make quick decisions on severance packages or on what to do with their retirement accounts if they lose their jobs. As you can see, it's important for you to start helping the media come up with news angles that will interest their audience as they create their stories.

As you become more familiar with the media and as contacts begin calling you on a regular basis as a source for stories or interviews, they'll begin to rely on you more and more to ensure that they are hitting the key points that their audience wants to know. They'll ask you for your feedback on a story angle. Time and time again, when I have gone into the newsroom to prepare for an interview, people there are in the process of writing out my questions. Many times they'll ask me to review the story angle to make sure

I'm knowledgeable on it and that it's a topic I think their audience will find of interest.

MEDIA ACTION POINTS

✔ When speaking to the media, think of ways to make a statistic meaningful to your audience.

✔ Be prepared to help "guide" the media toward the best story angle for your interview.

GETTING INVITED BACK

Let's say that you've completed your first interview and your producer and the anchors comment that you did well. Now it's time to position yourself for your next appearance. Do you want to know the secret to getting in the media on a frequent basis? Let me be honest with you. It won't happen if you sit at your desk and wait for the phone to ring. You have to work proactively to create your next opportunity. Here's the easiest way to do it. Once you've appeared on a television or radio program and your producers say you did a great job, begin sending in questions they can ask you in future interviews. This is the best way to put yourself in a position to be interviewed again and again as a financial expert on news programs. Instead of giving producers the burden of trying to think of topics for you to discuss on the air, suggest topics yourself. The easier you make it on the producers, directors, and writers, the more likely they are to use your questions and use you as their regular contact.

Let me be candid about this. Creating these questions and topics will require some of your time. But think about it. This is one of the best marketing opportunities you will ever have, and all it takes is a little time to prepare your material and then to show up to do the interview. In addition, if you come up with your own topics, you'll be deciphering complex financial topics in an easy-to-understand way for the audience while at the same time conveying the exact message you want to deliver to your ideal prospects. You're creating a win-win relationship.

GETTING SCRIPTED

When you appear on television or on radio, typically you'll know ahead of time what questions you'll be asked. Before your interview, the producer will hand you a copy of a script to look over. The script shows the exact steps that will take place during your interview—how you'll be introduced, the questions you'll be asked, and what the news anchor will say to end your interview.

Once you receive the script, look it over carefully and make sure your name is spelled correctly and your title and company name are listed accurately. How this information appears on the script is exactly how it will appear on the TV screen when you're being introduced or exactly what the radio DJ will say when introducing you. If there is something wrong, politely speak up and let them know. It's far better to catch a mistake or a misspelling now instead of saying something right before you're about to start the interview, when people will have to scramble to make the change. When it's showtime, you want to be relaxed and focused on doing a great interview. You don't want to be nervous or upset at yourself for not correcting a problem.

As I discussed, when the media call you to do an interview, a script already will be prepared for you. However, at other times you need to create interview ideas that you feel would interest their audience. It's time for you to learn how to write scripts that the television and radio programs can use easily. The secret is to write your own script in such a way that it blends in well with the style of the news program on which you're appearing. That way it will sound as if the media contacts wrote it themselves.

FIVE STEPS TO WRITING YOUR SCRIPTS

1. *Select a timely and relevant topic that will interest the media's audience.* Here are some places to get topic ideas for your scripts:

- Financial web sites
- Newsletters that your company sends out to clients
- Common questions your clients have
- Financial topics or products that are in the news

2. Write an introduction that captures people's attention. Typically the introduction begins with one or two sentences about the topic to capture the audience's attention. Then you are introduced as the expert who is here to explain what the topic means to the audience. For example, here's a sample script introduction:

> Wall Street finished another roller-coaster week. With all the volatility, many investors close to retirement are worried that they may not have their money in the right places. Here to bring some common sense to a complex issue is our financial expert (your name) of (your company name). Good (morning/afternoon/evening), (your name)!

3. *Write your questions based on the topic you've selected.* As you write these questions, imagine what the average viewer or listener at home might want to know about the topic. Then build your questions to allow you to cover the key points to help them best understand the topic. One strategy to writing good questions for anchors is to make them sound conversational. Put together the sentence exactly as the anchor would talk. You never want questions to sound scripted. Well-written questions sound as if the anchor just thought of it off the top of her head. That's the style you want to use. Here are some sample questions:

> "(Your name), let's get to this. How are people that are close to retirement affected by dips in the stock market?"
>
> "(Your name), what can investors do to protect themselves?"
>
> "Okay, (your name), let's say that someone is going to retire next month. What are the steps they should take to be ready to retire?"
>
> "What are you telling your clients to do right now?"

Let's briefly examine how these questions were written. You want to write your questions so that they convey urgency about a particular financial issue, yet sound conversational and to the point. The last sample question is of my favorites that I regularly include in the scripts I send to the media. From the audience's perspective, when the anchor asks, "What are you telling your clients to do right now?" it appears that she is putting you on the spot to see if the answers you're giving now are different from what you say to your clients in real life. That's why this question is so powerful. It lets you showcase how you work with clients.

As financial professionals, you and I know that every investor is different. Each has unique goals, a different risk tolerance, time frame, and so on. In answering this question the key is to phrase your answer in a way that captures the attention of the right people.

My response would be: "(Interviewer name), when prospective clients come into my office, they typically share with me that they're concerned about the stock market and they feel they are not aware of all their investment options. For retired clients, they usually want more income than they're getting from their bank CD's, so we discuss some higher-paying, income-producing investments that work well. If clients have a few years until retirement, we'll discuss ways to grow the portfolio but with less risk than the overall stock market. I have found that each person's situation is different. So the key is to work with a qualified financial professional."

Let's examine the points I made in my response:

- Retired clients all want more income.
- Most retired investors have CDs at the bank.
- I communicated that I understand the concerns of retired investors.
- Most pre-retired investors want their portfolios to grow but with less risk.
- Investors continually are trying to stay informed about all their investment options.
- I communicated that I also understand the concerns of pre-retired investors.

The key to answering questions like this is to give some information but say it in a way that leaves the audience wanting more. Doing this will cause viewers to want to contact you to find out the specifics; that leads to a new appointment for you. When you get asked open-ended questions, take advantage of them. Use them to describe how you work with clients and make the point that new clients are coming to your office every day to meet with you. This lets people know that they may be able to work with you. Remember what we discussed earlier about answering each question in a way that makes sense to the average person. That's what these questions set you up to do. In the last question, you described how you work with clients. You said that your clients don't worry a lot because you watch their money closely. Then, just when it looked as if you were about to try to promote yourself on the air, you did just the opposite. Instead of telling people to call you right now, you said for them to find another professional to work with. By answering the question this way, you come across as unbiased and somewhat hard to get.

Ideal prospects often are drawn to working with you if you convey a subtle attitude that you're content with your existing group of ideal clients and you're not begging for new business. Clients with money want to work with advisors who are as successful as they are. And most accomplished people don't brag about themselves. If you overly promote yourself as you appear in the media, it actually can work against you by turning off prospective clients. Now, let me make a critical differentiation here. As you're working to *break into* the media, you should overly promote yourself. Once you're being interviewed *in* the media, you should downplay yourself. Let the media do the work of promoting you on the air. You just show up and present yourself as a trustworthy and knowledgeable financial professional with whom the media enjoys working. Maintaining this attitude will work to attract more ideal clients than you ever thought possible.

   4. *For television, create your graphics for the screen.* Briefly summarize your answers into bullet points that can appear on the screen as you're speaking. Doing this complements your interview by making it look very polished. It also gives you a way to remember the answer to the question in case you forget.

   5. *Write a tagline to end the interview.* The tagline is the part where the anchor thanks you for appearing and provides a way for the audience to contact you for more information. Here are three sample taglines:

   TAG: Thanks, (your first name). If you have question for (your first name), you can call the station for his contact information.

TAG: (Your first name), thanks for the great information. (Your first name) will return on (day and time) with more financial tips. If you'd like (your first name) to speak to your company or organization, log on to our web site at (station web site address) and click on (wherever your information is located) for his contact information.

TAG: Thanks, (your first name). (Your first name) will return on (day and time) with more financial tips that you can use. In the meantime, if you have a question for (your first name), log on to (station website address) and click on (wherever your information is located) for his contact information.

The following are four sample scripts covering a wide range of topics that you can use as a guide to writing your own. Some of this information was taken from msn.com.

Sample Script 1

SCRIPT FOR (Date and Time)
TOPIC: 5 TIPS FOR HANDLING AN INHERITANCE

INTRO: Receiving an inheritance can be an emotionally complicated issue. It's sometimes difficult to figure out what you should do with the unexpected money. Here today with some tips on how to best handle an unexpected windfall is our Channel 4 Financial Expert Joe Smith, from ABC Financial. Good morning, Joe!

GRAPHICS:
1. Find out exactly how much you're receiving
2. Make a list of your goals
3. Decide exactly how much to splurge
4. Set aside an emergency fund
5. Create an investment strategy

QUESTION: Joe, we're talking about inheritances today, but wouldn't these tips apply to any large sum of money you receive?

ANSWER: Certainly. Whether you're receiving an inheritance, a court settlement, an award, or any other substantial lump sum, these are some good tips for you to follow.

QUESTION: Your first tip is to figure out how much you're really going to receive. How do you do that?

ANSWER: In the case of an inheritance, you usually don't receive a one-time check from the executor of the estate. Instead, you'll receive bits and pieces of different investments and insurance benefits. Before you make any plans with the money, you need to determine exactly how much you'll be receiving and how much you'll be paying in taxes on the money.

QUESTION: Your second tip is to make a list of both your short- and long-term financial goals. Why is that so important?

ANSWER: Once you've made that list, you need to assign dollar amounts to each goal. Then you can compare that list with the amount of money you'll be receiving. The reason this is important is that often when people receive a large lump sum of money, they are tempted to spend it all on short-term goals, like remodeling their home or going on a pricey vacation. But you may end up having a difficult time meeting long-term goals like retirement or your children's education, and if you invest a lump sum now you'll have a better chance at achieving those long-term goals down the road.

QUESTION: You're bound to splurge with some of the money you receive, right?

ANSWER: Sure, but the important thing is to decide in advance exactly how much you're willing to splurge. After looking over that list of goals you've created, decide how much you can really afford to spend, then set that money aside in a different, liquid account. That way you can go and buy that new car or whatever, but when the money is gone, it's gone, and you've protected the money you're using for your long-term goals.

QUESTION: What about setting aside an emergency fund?

ANSWER: One of your biggest priorities should be to set up an emergency fund, if you don't have one already. It should be enough to cover three to six months of your usual expenses. That way you're protected in case of an emergency or short-term job loss. Put this money into a money market account or other safe but liquid investment.

QUESTION: Your final tip is to establish an investment strategy for your long-term goals. Why is that so important?

ANSWER: It's very important to have a strategy for your investments, to make sure you'll achieve those long-term goals. You need to know how to diversify the money and what kinds of returns you'll need in order to grow the money enough to meet your goals. The best way to set up such a strategy is to meet with a qualified financial advisor. An advisor can walk you through your goals, risk tolerance, and investment experience and put together a plan for you.

TAG: Joe, thanks for the great information. Joe will return on Monday at 10 with more financial tips. If you'd like Joe to speak to your company or organization, log on to our web site at Channel 4.com and click on News for his contact information.

Sample Script 2

SCRIPT FOR (Date and Time)
TOPIC: 5 TIPS FOR THE BEGINNING INVESTOR

INTRO: Do you want to start investing, but don't know where to begin? Are you afraid of jumping into the stock market and making a mistake? To help make sense of it all for the beginning investor is Channel 4 Financial Expert Joe Smith from ABC Financial to give us five tips on successfully getting started in the investment game. Good evening, Joe!

GRAPHICS:
1. Cover your risks
2. Contribute to your 401(k)
3. Pay off credit cards
4. Set up emergency fund
5. Think about your goals and timeframe

QUESTION: Joe, how important is insurance when someone is getting started with investing?

ANSWER: Very important. The first thing you need to do is cover your risks. Make sure you have health insurance to cover your medical bills if you become ill or have an accident. Make sure you have disability coverage to provide you with income if you have an accident and are unable to work. You need property and liability insurance to protect your home and belongings. And you need life insurance if you have dependents who rely on your income.

QUESTION: One easy strategy is to invest through a 401(k) plan. How much should you contribute to that?

ANSWER: Your 401(k) is a great tool for you to get started. You should definitely contribute up to the full amount that is matched by your employer. That money is deducted from your paycheck before taxes are paid, and it grows tax-deferred until you withdraw the money. If you're not contributing up to the full employer match amount, you're throwing away free money from your company.

QUESTION: What about paying off credit cards—should that be a priority?

ANSWER: Definitely. The third thing you should do is work to pay off all your credit card debt. After all, if you owe $2,000 on a credit card charging you 18 percent, paying that card off can save you quite a bit of interest. Paying off debt also give you more flexibility with your money because it frees up your cash flow and give you the chance to take advantage of opportunities that may come your way.

QUESTION: What about stashing away money for emergencies—how much should you keep on hand?

ANSWER: The next thing you should do is set up an emergency fund. You should have three to six months of living expenses in a readily accessible savings account. That way if something unexpected comes up, whether it's a major medical bill, a car repair, or a job layoff, you're covered. When you are forced to take money from this account, make repaying it a top priority.

QUESTION: What's your last tip?

ANSWER: You need to think about your goals and your time frame before you can set up a plan to achieve those goals. Many people fail to think through those two things and just start buying stocks or mutual funds without any idea of what they want the money for. You've got to think through your goals, and how long you have to achieve those goals, before you can figure out how to obtain them. A financial advisor can help you create a customized plan to achieve your goals.

TAG: Thanks, Joe. Joe will return on Friday at 10 with more financial tips that you can use. In the meantime, if you have question for Joe, log on to Channel 4.com and click on News for his contact information.

Sample Script 3

SCRIPT FOR (Date and Time)
TOPIC: 4 TIPS FOR RETIRING WITH A BEAT-UP PORTFOLIO

INTRO: After any financial downturn in the stock market, many people worry how they can retire when their portfolio suffers big losses. While the future may look bleak to those facing retirement soon, it is possible to still have the retirement you've imagined. Here to explain is Channel 4 Financial Expert Joe Smith with ABC Financial. Good afternoon, Joe!

GRAPHICS:
1. Downsize your home
2. Plan on less income
3. Work longer at a job you enjoy
4. Consider an overseas retirement

QUESTION: For people facing retirement in a few years, how can their home equity help them reach their goals?

ANSWER: For many people, their home is their single biggest asset as they face retirement. This creates a potential problem because of the lack of diversification. Although home prices have been rising quickly over the past several years, that pace may slow in the future. If you have more than 40 percent of your assets in your home equity, you may want to consider diversifying that to take advantage of higher returns elsewhere.

If some or all of your children have already moved out on their own, consider downsizing to a smaller home with a lower mortgage. Lower-priced homes tend to sustain their value better, since there is always demand for smaller, "starter" homes for new families. And any gain you capture from the sale, up to (fill in current amount), may be tax-free. You can then invest that profit in a more diversified portfolio.

QUESTION: A few years ago, we used to plan on making 12 percent or more on our investments. Now many financial planners are saying to plan on only 7 to 8 percent returns. What else should we expect?

ANSWER: Well, you're right to plan on lower returns than we were making in the 90s. However, what many planners aren't telling you is that you can also plan on spending less in retirement. In the past, we've heard that we should plan on replacing 70 to 80 percent of our preretirement income, or even as much as 100 percent for some people. But the truth is, after major monthly expenses like mortgages, college tuition, and retirement savings are no longer a factor in retirement, many people can happily live on about half of what they were making before. It's great if you can afford to replace 80 percent of your income. But don't hesitate to make a "Plan B" where you're living off of a little less. You may find it's quite doable.

QUESTION: What about working longer and retiring later?

ANSWER: That's definitely a good idea to help you reach your retirement goals. Just make sure that you're working longer at a job you enjoy. That may mean making a career change. You may have been working long hours at a job you dislike, thinking that if you can sock away the money now you could retire early. Now that your 401(k) has lost half its value, you're looking at working there twice as long as you'd planned. Instead of working more years at a job you don't like, you should be looking for a job you enjoy, so that those extra years will be rewarding instead of feeling unbearable.

QUESTION: Joe, you say that retiring overseas can be a cheaper option. Explain.

ANSWER: Many people consider retiring overseas, especially if they don't have close family ties to keep them in the country. Many other countries, like Ireland, Costa Rica, and even some islands of the Bahamas, may offer a much lower cost of living than here in the U.S., including reduced costs of prescription drugs. If you've always dreamed of living in a foreign land, retirement may be the best time to do so.

QUESTION: Any last tips?

ANSWER: To give you the best chance for success, it's important to work with a professional advisor who specializes in retirement planning. Someone who's helped a lot of other people retire. So it's best to work with a qualified financial advisor.

TAG: Thanks, Joe! Joe will be back on Monday at 10 with more tips on planning your retirement. In the meantime, if you have a question for Joe, log onto our web site at Channel 4.com, and click on News for his contact information.

Sample Script 4

SCRIPT FOR (Date and Time)
TOPIC: TRIMMING YOUR TAXES BEFORE YEAR-END

INTRO: This time of year, few of us are thinking about our income taxes. But there are steps to take now which can trim your tax bill for this year. Joining us today with five ways to save on taxes is Channel 4 Financial Expert Joe Smith, of ABC Financial.

GRAPHICS:
Defer income
Use tax laws to ease pain of market losses
Medical expenses
Make an early mortgage payment
Noncash charitable donations

QUESTION: How can deferring income help with taxes?

ANSWER: Basically, if there's any income that you don't have to take in this calendar year, deferring it into next can help you save on income taxes for this year. Plus, since tax brackets are adjusted annually for inflation, deferring until next year may give you a small tax break by pushing some income into a lower bracket.

QUESTION: Let's say that someone has lost money in some of their investments. How can those losses help you save on taxes?

ANSWER: Generally speaking, capital losses offset capital gains on a dollar-for-dollar basis. You can use up to (fill in amount) of losses that exceed your capital gains to offset your ordinary income. In other words, if you've lost $5,000 and made $2,000 in capital gains, you can use the $3,000 difference to offset your income for the year. If you have more than (fill in amount) in losses after you've included your gains, the excess can be carried over to next year.

QUESTION: Now, I know you can deduct medical expenses only if they exceed a certain percentage of your income. But if you haven't reached that amount, what can you do?

ANSWER: Well, if you know that you have some medical treatment that you need in the future, you may want to try to schedule it before year-end. Elective surgery, orthodontic work, or even medical premiums can be moved to this year if necessary so that you can meet the amount needed to deduct the expenses.

QUESTION: What about making an early mortgage payment?

ANSWER: Many people are a little strapped for cash in December with the holiday season. But here's an option to consider. If you can get your shopping bills paid early and make your January mortgage payment or property tax payment before December 31, you'll be able to claim the interest on your tax deduction for this year, which can help on taxes.

QUESTION: Many people are making charitable contributions this year. How can noncash donations help with your taxes?

ANSWER: Giving away clothing, furniture, or other items to your church or a favorite charity before January 1 will generally allow you to deduct the fair market value of your contribution. But you have to get a receipt. Without one you can't claim the deduction.

QUESTION: Joe, do you have a final tip?

ANSWER: Whenever you deal with tax issues, remember that it's always best to consult a tax advisor. They can tell you what strategy is best for your particular situation.

TAG: Great information, Joe. Joe will return on Friday at 10 with more financial tips. If you'd like Joe to speak to your company or organization, log onto our web site at Channel4.com, and click on News for his contact information.

MEDIA ACTION POINTS

✔ Choose relevant and newsworthy topics for your news scripts.

✔ Write a two- to three-sentence introduction for the anchor.

✔ Break your topic into four to five questions the anchor can ask you. Write questions you think your audience would want to have answered.

✔ Write answers to the questions so you can use them to practice before the interview.

✔ If the television station uses graphics during interviews, consider summarizing your answers as bullet points and including them in the script, so that the producers can display them on the screen as you're speaking.

✔ Write a tagline that includes how viewers or listeners can contact you for more information.

✔ *Note:* The best way to send scripts is by e-mail to your producer.

By developing your own scripts, you give yourself the opportunity to speak on topics that you are knowledgeable about and that you specialize in. By speaking on topics that you enjoy, you'll be much more relaxed, and that will come across to the audience. What you talk about on the air also will help define the type of financial professional you are. For example, if each time you are interviewed you discuss the stock market and individual stocks, viewers will get the impression that you are a broker who focuses primarily on selling stocks. If you speak on topics ranging from education planning to insurance policies, viewers will begin to think of you as a professional advisor with a broad knowledge of financial issues.

The best way to write successful scripts is to connect the subject to the concerns and interests of your ideal prospects. For example, if you're discussing the stock market, you could say, "The stock market has been volatile. Here's what I say to my clients who are a few years from retirement . . ." (or whatever types of clients you work with). By saying this, you've taken a topic that has very broad appeal, answered the question, and tied your answer to the viewers with whom you would like to work.

MEDIA ACTION POINTS

✔ As you appear in the media, discuss the topics that you want to become known as the expert in.

✔ In your media appearances, discuss topics that will appeal to your ideal prospects.

LEVERAGING THE NEWSPAPER

The newspaper is another excellent media component to help position yourself as the financial expert in your local area. Unlike television and radio, where you are interviewed for only a few minutes and then you're off the air, being quoted in a newspaper story can help keep your name and company name in front of people for a longer time. Although some people simply glance through the newspaper, others read and reread articles they find of interest. You want your quotes in the business articles to capture readers' attention.

Here are the two primary ways to begin positioning yourself as the expert through your local newspapers:

1. Let editors/reporters know that you're a source they can call on for their stories.

2. Approach editors about submitting a guest article to the publication.

You can contact editors of local newspapers and introduce yourself as a local financial expert that their reporters can call on for expert commentary on their news stories either by sending an introductory fax or e-mail or by calling directly. I have found that faxes and e-mails are the best way to go, since both can be read when the editors have time; unexpected phone calls interrupt editors' busy schedules. Let the editors know that you are readily accessible and that if you're in a meeting when a reporter calls, you will return the call very quickly. The editors will forward your name to the reporters who cover the appropriate topics, and they'll keep your name and number as a potential source.

MEDIA ACTION POINTS

✔ Send introductory faxes or e-mails to local editors, letting them know that you're available to comment on financial stories.

✔ Let them know that you're easily accessible and will return calls quickly, and briefly outline your expertise.

Another way to position yourself as an expert is to ask editors if you could submit a guest article on a financial topic that you feel would be of great interest to readers. (You pick the topic.) Ask if the paper would consider running the article on a "space-available" basis. That means the article will be printed if some space needs to be filled in the newspaper on any given day. Let editors know that you feel your article would provide timely and beneficial information for readers, because more and more people have a desire for easy-to-understand financial information that they can apply to their own lives. Emphasize that the article will be informational only and will not be a sales pitch. (This is a key point to make. Most editors have been approached by financial professionals who tried to submit guest articles that were nothing more than sales pitches. Because of bad experiences in the past, editors may be a bit hesitant. However, you can overcome this concern with your professional approach.) If an editor is interested, ask how long the article needs to be and when he'd like you to get the article to him. Say you'll be back in touch as soon as the article is completed.

Once you've been given the green light from an editor to put a guest column together, you have to decide whether you want to write it yourself or have the article ghostwritten (someone else writes the article for you but you put your name on it so it appears that you wrote it). As I consult with financial professionals, I have discovered that many have great ideas they want to share with the public, but they may lack the interest, time, or ability to develop and write an article. That's where ghostwriting comes in. If you're associated with a national financial services company, check with its marketing or corporate communications department to see if the firm offers a byline financial column program. That's another name for columns that are prewritten and legally approved by the compliance department. All you do is insert your name and contact information into it and send it to the media. It's a very easy process. If that option isn't available to you, then it's time for you to find a ghostwriter to complete your article.

Here are four ways for you to complete your guest article:

1. Go to your broker-dealer. See if the firm has prewritten and preapproved financial articles you can send to the newspaper.

2. Go to the Internet. Use your favorite search engine and type in the following keywords: "financial ghostwriting," "ghostwritten articles," or "ghostwriting." Then review the entries that pop up, and contact a few to get more information and pricing. Then determine if one of the writers might fit your needs.

3. Go to your friends. Think of people you know who are good writers and see if they would be available to create an article for you.

4. Go to college. Call your local college's English or business department and find out if there are professors who do freelance writing.

Whether you decide to write the guest article yourself or hire a ghostwriter, here are the six steps to getting started:

1. *Select a timely and interesting topic.* For example, think about the time of year and address an issue that people are thinking about, such as taxes or college expenses. Toward the end of the year, articles about how to pay for Christmas gifts and still keep your retirement on track are popular. Also, the end of each calendar year and the beginning of the next are normal times for people to retire. Consider topics such as: What You Need to Know Before You Retire, or Thinking About Retirement? Here's What to Know About Your Retirement Money.

2. *Do your research.* As a financial professional, you already have a great deal of knowledge on most financial topics. Now it's time to tap into your internal resource guide. Write out the key points you

want to make. Then add some statistics to the article, such as people's average retirement age, the average life expectancy for men and women, or the percentage of people who are truly financially independent when they retire.

3. *Start writing.* Most articles are written in such a way that the average fifth-grader can read and understand them. Use simple, direct language and eliminate excessive words. Write the article in the present tense, identifying people's concerns and then offering tangible financial alternatives or action steps for them to consider taking now.

4. *Proofread and reread.* Once your article is complete, read it over several times and double-check any statistics or numbers. Then make sure your article is the length requested by the editor. Have several people read through the article and give you their first impressions about how smoothly it flows, how easy it is to read, and whether it is bogged down with technical financial jargon. You want to make sure it sounds conversational.

5. *Include your tagline.* At the end of your guest article, you should include some brief information on how readers can contact you. The tagline is critical because it offers the readers a direct way to reach you. As most editors realize that you're providing a valuable service to their readers, they will let you put your contact information in the tagline. However, if an editor frowns on that idea, insist that he at least print your name, title, company name, and where you are located. Here are two tagline examples:

> *Preferred option:* "(Your first name) is a financial advisor with (your company name) in (city name). He specializes in retirement and investment planning for his clients. He can be reached at (phone number) or by e-mail at (your e-mail address)."

> *Other option:* "(Your first name) is a financial advisor with (your company name) in (city name)."

6. *Send the article to the editor.* I have learned that when you submit an article, you should not expect it to be published just as you wrote it. Instead, you want to ask for feedback and encourage the editor to give you ideas on any changes that might make the article even better. Keep in mind the title of the person to whom you're sending your article: editor. The very definition suggests that editors are used to modifying and enhancing the writings of others—adding phrases to articles, cutting sentences that don't fit, and tweaking things. That's what they do all day with their reporters' stories, and they will do the same with your article. When you e-mail or fax your guest article to the editor, a cover letter should say:

> Dear (editor's first name):
>
> As we discussed, here is the first draft of the guest article on (your topic name), which I feel will be of great interest to your readers, to be run on a space-available basis. Please read it over and e-mail or call me with any changes or edits. I'll make any necessary changes immediately and get it right back to you.
>
> Thanks for your time in reviewing this.
>
> Sincerely,
>
> (your name)
>
> (your phone numbers)

Let me let you in on a little secret. When you approach editors with a humble attitude and ask for advice on how you can write a better article, you are far more likely to get your article published than the financial professional who is egotistical or arrogant about his or her writing. The media business is a game of power. Always let your media contacts be in control or feel as if they are. Always ask for their opinions and what they think you should do to improve. Financial professionals who understand this fundamental media principle will have a higher likelihood of success than those who don't. It's that simple.

Once the editor sends you changes to be made, make them right away and resubmit the article for printing. Also, let the editor know that you would like to have your picture appear with the article.

Here are four sample byline financial columns that were written by my broker-dealer and that I used in my local area to get published.

Byline Column 1: Target Market: Pre-Retired

DELAYING RETIREMENT
By Joe Smith

What do you want to do in retirement? Are you looking forward to spending more time with family? Do you want to golf or travel? We all dream of having the time to do what we love in retirement. But when will you be able to retire and begin that new phase in your life?

According to the Employee Benefit Research Institute, more and more baby boomers say they'll retire after age 65, and 70% of all employees now plan to work at least part-time after they retire from their current careers. Furthermore, the current economic environment will force 2.3 million U.S. households to delay retirement—according to a recent survey by Intuit, Inc.

So how can you know how much money you'll need in retirement and when you can afford to stop working? These questions can be complicated and confusing. But there are several tips that can help you plan wisely and achieve your retirement goals.

Why Delay Retirement?
People are delaying retirement for many reasons. According to *Consumer Reports*, those reasons include recent market downturns, the weak job market, and the fact that traditional pension plans are almost a thing of the past. However, as more and more people who are living longer and in better health are discovering, working longer can offer some advantages you should consider.

First of all, delaying retirement can allow your retirement savings to continue growing, and may also allow insurance benefits, like health coverage, to pick up expenses that Medicare won't. Second, if you delay withdrawals from tax-deferred accounts, your money will have more time to grow tax-free. Finally, for every month past your full retirement age that you keep working, your Social Security benefits increase by a certain percentage, with some restrictions.

Before You Retire
Before you retire, you should work with a professional to create a comprehensive financial plan, so that you'll know how much money you will need and when you will need it. When you have a plan, you can begin to work realistically toward your goals.

- **Be specific.** Set your retirement goals in writing. Include when you want to retire, where you'll live, and what you plan to do, whether it's travel or other hobbies. Be as specific as possible so that you'll have a clear picture of what it will take to achieve those goals.

- **Stretch savings.** Stretch your savings by as much as possible by withdrawing from taxable accounts first. This allows your tax-deferred accounts to grow for a longer period of time. You should also consider cutting expenses before retirement, like downsizing your home.

- **Evaluate insurance.** Look into buying long-term care insurance. If you become unable to work and require special assistance such as nursing home care, long-term care insurance can help bridge the gap between your savings and the high expenses of such treatment.

- **Rebalance.** Reallocate your portfolio to ensure that you have the right balance of stocks, bonds, and cash to meet your goals. Be sure that your allocation also reflects your risk tolerance.

- **Know your IRAs.** Don't invest too much in traditional IRAs, since these accounts require you to begin withdrawals at age $70\frac{1}{2}$. Consider investing in Roth IRAs instead, which don't require you to take a distribution in your lifetime. 401(k)s also don't require distributions as long as you are working.

- **Other options.** Instead of delaying retirement indefinitely, think about working part time or retiring over time, which may help you adjust more readily, both financially and emotionally, to your new stage of life.

When Is the Right Time for Retirement?

How will you know when you've saved enough so that your assets will last through your life? It requires some careful planning to answer this question. For example, let's look at a 60-year-old working man who saved $411,440 for retirement. He is saving $24,000 per year and getting an average investment return of 8%. If his retirement goal is $4,000 of income per month, with Social Security payments of $1,640 per month beginning at age 65, here's how he will do:

If he retires at age 62, this man's money will run out by age 77. If he retires a mere three years later, at age 65, his money will last until he's 90. If he retires at age 67, he'll be covered until he is 102 years old. As this example illustrates, a few additional years of working can dramatically stretch your savings and allow you to be covered throughout your lifetime.

Get Help

There are many aspects to consider when planning for your retirement. A financial advisor can help you create a comprehensive retirement plan to help you meet both your long- and short-term goals.

###

Joe Smith is a financial advisor with ABC Financial in Chicago. He specializes in retirement and investment planning for individuals and business owners. Joe can be reached at 555-1234 or at jsmith@abcfinancial.com.

Byline Column 2: Target Market: Self-Employed
FINANCIAL PLANNING FOR THE SELF-EMPLOYED
By Joe Smith

Independent contractors, whether they're mechanics, accountants, plumbers, or writers, all leave the corporate world in order to pursue their own flexible hours and their own dreams. The ranks of the self-employed are definitely growing. But if you want to join them, you'd better have a financial plan. While working for yourself does allow you some new freedoms, it also presents unique financial challenges. Here are some important considerations:

- **Setting up your business.** First of all, you'll need to decide whether to be a sole proprietor or to choose a form of incorporation, such as a C corporation, subchapter S, or limited liability company. For self-employed individuals, sole proprietorship is the most frequent choice, since it's less complicated and less expensive than incorporating. However, you may want to consider incorporation if you have concerns about legal liabilities, since the various types of incorporation can offer limited liability protection. As you make this decision, consult with professional advisors who can help you choose the best option for you.
- **Managing cash flow.** As an independent contractor, you'll probably be dealing with an uneven cash flow. Since you're not receiving a regular, scheduled paycheck, you might wind up ahead one month and virtually penniless the next. To make sure that you always have cash when you need it, you should develop a budget and a financial plan that allow for

swings in income. Take your yearly income and figure out an average of how much monthly revenue you can count on. Then use that average and subtract our your monthly expenses. During months that you make more, save the extra in an interest-earning savings account or money market account, which you can draw from during months you have little or no income. You should also consider paying yourself a salary and maintaining separate accounts for your personal and business cash. Otherwise, you may face complications come tax time.

- **Get the necessary insurance.** First, find out whether you can obtain coverage from your spouse's benefit plan, if he or she is working. Otherwise, you'll need to provide your own health, disability and life insurance.

    Health: Unfortunately, many self-employed individuals choose to ignore this need when they start their own businesses. According to the National Association for the Self-employed, more than 60% of the 41 million uninsured in America are in households headed by a self-employed individual. If you can't get health insurance through your working spouse's benefits, consider opening a medical savings account (MSA). With an MSA, you can take a tax deduction for the money you deposit into the account to pay for out-of-pocket medical expenses associated with a high-deductible healthcare policy. If you don't spend all the money in the MSA, it can remain there and earn interest tax-deferred.

    Disability: It can be difficult for the self-employed to find a good, affordable disability policy to replace lost income, since disability insurers usually work with groups. One option may be to join an industry trade association or alumni organization that offers access to disability insurance.

    Life: Life insurance can provide your family with the money to pay off your mortgage or send your kids to college if you die. You can choose from several types of life insurance, from term insurance (death benefit only) to cash value (cash accumulation and death benefit) to combinations of the two. However, it may be difficult to obtain life insurance on your own if you have medical issues that often aren't questioned under a group plan.

- **Retirement savings.** 401(k)s may be too complicated and expensive for the self-employed. Instead, look into tax-deductible vehicles, such as Keogh plans and simplified employee pension plans (SEPs), as well as traditional individual retirement accounts (IRAs.) There are also nondeductible options, like Roth IRAs and annuities. If you incorporate as a small business, consider setting up a savings incentive match plan for employees (SIMPLE) IRA. SIMPLE IRAs were created for companies with fewer than 100 employees (including self-employed workers) with no other qualified plan. SIMPLEs offer both income tax-deferred savings and employer-matching flexibility.

- **Managing taxes.** As an independent contractor, you won't have an employer taking out taxes from your paychecks. You're responsible for paying your own income and Social Security taxes, so it's vital that you put aside the money to cover taxes from each payment you receive, before you spend that income. Otherwise, when it's time to file your quarterly estimated taxes or annual return, you may not have enough to cover your bill. The good news is that the self-employed may be eligible for certain tax breaks. You may be able to deduct all of the following: contributions to retirement plans, health insurance premiums, auto expenses, travel costs, meals, entertainment, and office-related expenses. Always be sure to keep all of your receipts throughout the year, so you can claim every possible deduction at tax time.

It can be both intimidating and exciting to be self-employed. No matter what type of business you own, consider meeting with a qualified financial advisor who can help you manage your finances as you pursue success.

###

Joe Smith is a financial advisor with ABC Financial in Chicago. He specializes in retirement and investment planning for individuals and business owners. Joe can be reached at 555-1234 or at jsmith@abcfinancial.com.

Byline Column 3: Target Market: Pre-retired
WHEN PLANNING FOR RETIREMENT, EXPECT THE UNEXPECTED
By Joe Smith

Even if you think you've saved enough money for retirement, you may want to double-check. According to the most recent Retirement Confidence Survey, conducted by the nonprofit American Savings Education Council (ASEC), 19% of current retirees say their overall standard of living is worse than they expected when they retired. (Source: ASEC survey, www.asec.org.)

On average, respondents to the survey reported that they had retired several years earlier than planned, often due to unexpected reasons like a health problem or company downsizing. The idea of retiring early may sound appealing, but if you were expecting a few more years of steady income, you may not be prepared financially for an early retirement. The good news is that you may be able to avoid such problems if you take the time now to prepare for the costs of retirement.

Prepare for Unplanned Events

As you figure out how much money you need in retirement, don't limit yourself to your basic monthly expenses, like housing, utility bills, transportation, and groceries. Also keep in mind all the possible future events that could occur during retirement.

For example, consider how your finances would be affected by an expensive medical emergency or the long-term costs of staying in a nursing home. ASEC survey findings show that there are several other financial issues retirees often fail to consider:

- Health care costs are rising and Medicare coverage is decreasing.
- Cost-of-living expenses are often higher than expected.
- Social Security and pension benefits may be lower than anticipated.
- Investments may not have performed as well as expected.

Know What You'll Need

If you don't want to feel the financial pinch in retirement, you need to get an accurate picture of how much income you'll have in retirement. To do this, add up the income you expect to receive annually from all sources, including your employer-sponsored retirement plan, Social Security benefits, your personal investment portfolio, and your individual retirement account (IRA), if applicable.

After you've figured out your retirement income, compare it to the income you expect to be making just before you retire. If you hope to maintain your standard of living when you retire, most experts suggest you'll need a retirement income that's at least 70% to 80% of your preretirement income.

Supercharge Your Nest Egg

Once you've crunched the numbers, you may find that you have a shortfall. To make up for it, first make sure to contribute the maximum to your IRA and employer-sponsored retirement plan.

After you've contributed the maximum to your tax-deferred accounts, consider saving in a taxable investment portfolio. While it can't offer the tax benefits of an IRA, a taxable portfolio can help you save additional funds for retirement. Remember, the most important step in saving for retirement is to save as much as possible as early as possible. That's because time is the most crucial component of compound interest, which gives your retirement savings a chance to grow not only from its original principal, but also on its growth in prior years.

Compound interest can more dramatically increase your savings the longer you stay invested and regularly add to your portfolio. For example, if you deposit $100 a month into an account that earns an average of 7% annually, your investment will grow to more than $17,600 in 10 years, and more than $52,300 in 20 years.

Take Steps to Prevent Future Problems

You can protect yourself against further unexpected financial problems in retirement by following these tips:

- **Evaluate your medical insurance coverage.** If your main source of health insurance in retirement will be Medicare, consider supplementing it through private insurance or your employer-sponsored insurance plan, if one is available.
- **Gain a firm understanding of cost-of-living expenses.** Your cost of living in retirement will likely depend on where you live, since some parts of the country are more expensive than others. If you'll be moving to a rural area in retirement, you may have a lower cost of living, while moving to a large urban area may mean higher costs.
- **Don't overestimate investment returns.** Trying to figure out your portfolio's rate of return can be complicated. Your professional financial advisor can help you gain a clearer picture of the potential risks and benefits of your investments.
- **Consider long-term care insurance.** Without this insurance, you could be financially devastated by an extended stay in a nursing home during retirement. A recent study conducted by the American Council of Life Insurers estimates

the average cost of a nursing home stay will reach more than $190,000 annually by 2030.

The younger you are when you buy long-term care insurance, the cheaper the coverage will be. Many insurance-industry experts suggest purchasing long-term care insurance before age 60 to lock in lower premiums. If you have concerns about potential health problems that could make you uninsurable, you may want to buy coverage even earlier.

- **Plan for a longer retirement.** Keep in mind that your savings may need to last many years past your retirement age. In the 1950s, the average life expectancy of Americans was less than 65. Today, the average American can expect to live almost until age 77, according to the U.S. Department of Health and Human Services.

Create a Plan that Will Last a Lifetime

As you plan your retirement strategy, be sure to consider a variety of life events and market conditions. Your qualified financial advisor can give you a better idea of how prepared you are, based on your current financial status and your future plans.

###

Joe Smith is a financial advisor with ABC Financial in Chicago. He specializes in retirement and investment planning for individuals and business owners. Joe can be reached at 555-1234 or at jsmith@abcfinancial.com.

Byline Column 4: Target Market: Women Investors
THE TIME IS RIPE FOR WOMEN CONSIDERING HOME OWNERSHIP
By Susan Smith

More and more women are purchasing homes. A recent survey conducted by the National Association of Realtors found that single women in America bought homes at more than twice the rate of single men. (Source: NAR press release.)

More single women are seeking to own their own homes, thanks in part to delayed marriages, strong careers, and a high divorce rate. Since current mortgage interest rates are remaining relatively low in most of the country, now may be an opportune time for women who are considering buying a new home.

Why Buy?

Besides the opportunity to take advantage of current low interest rates, buying a home today may also be a good investment. If you're currently renting, the money you pay to your landlord each month disappears, without giving you any return on your investment. If you buy, however, part of every mortgage payment you make adds to the equity of your home. The difference between the amount you owe on your mortgage and the appraised value of your property is your equity.

Owning your own home also allows you to deduct real estate taxes and mortgage loan interest from your federal income taxes. Your deduction will correspond to your tax bracket—the higher your tax bracket, the greater the savings.

Getting Started

Since buying a home is one of the biggest financial investments you'll ever make, make sure you know what you're getting into as you start the home-buying process. Keep in mind that a house is not a liquid investment. Depending on future market conditions, you may not be able to sell your house quickly.

Consider prequalifying for a mortgage before you start looking for a home, so that you'll know your price range. Take the time to compare mortgages, and get the best plan for your financial situation. Here are the most common types of mortgages:

- **Fixed-rate mortgages** offer a fixed interest rate for the entire term of the loan, usually 15 or 30 years. With a fixed-rate loan, you'll have the stability of equal monthly payments over the entire life of the loan.
- **Adjustable-rate mortgages (ARMs)** start out with an interest rate that is usually lower than those offered by fixed-rate loans, but then adjusts up or down periodically. The length of the loan usually varies from one year to 30 years.

Know the Costs

To pay the down payment and closing costs, you should try to save about 25% of your future home's purchase price. In certain cases—such as if you're single—it may be appropriate to buy after you've saved as little as 10% of the purchase price. If mortgage interest rates are low and you expect home prices to increase, you may want to consider this option.

Here's a closer look at some of the costs you can expect to pay when you buy a home:

- **Down payment.** Your goal should be to save as much as possible toward the purchase of your home. In most cases, you'll be able to gain more favorable terms on your loan if you have a larger down payment. If your down payment is less than 20%, you'll probably have to purchase private mortgage insurance (PMI), which can cost several hundred dollars annually.

- **Closing costs.** Closing costs are generally 3% to 6% of the home's purchase price, though these costs vary by state.
- **Other costs.** Don't forget to budget for other home-related expenses, such as comprehensive homeowners insurance, property taxes, utilities, and maintenance. When you find a home you like, ask for copies of the past two years of utility bills, so you can get a rough estimate of what you'll be paying.

Narrowing the Search

As you narrow the search for your home, you should first make some basic decisions about what you'll need. Decide how many bedrooms or bathrooms you want and what type of neighborhood you prefer. According to the National Association of Realtors, the biggest deciding factor for singles and families in the home-buying process is location—the neighborhood, price, and the distance to work, school, family, and friends.

You should also look into houses that fit your lifestyle. If you're single or childless, you may want to consider condominiums or townhouses, which generally have lower costs, more security, and lower maintenance than houses. On the other hand, if you have children, you may want to look for homes that provide ample space and other amenities for your family.

Rely on Professional Guidance

To the first-time home buyer, the process can seem complicated and confusing. A reputable real estate broker can help you navigate the selection and purchase process and help you with the closing. Talk to friends, relatives, and coworkers to get referrals, and then interview several agents. Consider finding an agent who's familiar with the neighborhoods you like.

It's also a good idea to talk to a qualified financial advisor to determine how a house purchase might affect your overall finances. Your professional financial advisor can help you decide which mortgage type and terms are best for your situation. Your advisor can also help make sure that you're saving enough toward other important financial goals, like retirement or a child's education.

###

Susan Smith is a financial advisor with XYZ Financial in New York City. She specializes in retirement and investment planning for individuals and business owners. Susan can be reached at 555-1234 or at ssmith@xyzfinancial.com.

MEDIA ACTION POINTS

✔ Ask an editor if you can write a guest article for his publication, to be run on a space-available basis. Explain that your article will provide timely information that would benefit his
   readers.

✔ If the editor agrees, ask about the word count and any other re-
   quirements.

✔ Decide whether you want to write the article yourself or have it
   ghostwritten, or find out if your company writes byline
   columns.

✔ If you write the column yourself, select a relevant and interesting
   topic and do the research.

✔ Write so that the average fifth-grader can understand your
   column.

✔ Include a tagline at the bottom of the article with biographical
   information and how you can be contacted.

✔ Have others proofread your article before you submit it.

✔ Ask for feedback from the editor once you've submitted the column, and make any recommended changes.

MAXIMIZING MAGAZINES

Unlike newspapers, which have to fill their pages on a daily basis,
most magazines are published only monthly. That means they have
a lot less space available for your story ideas or press releases. However, you shouldn't count them out entirely. Just think of them as a
bigger challenge. Some of the advisors I've consulted with have submitted guest articles to magazines in their local areas that significantly lifted their visibility and credibility. Depending on where

you're located, you'll be considering primarily three types of magazines: city, state, and national.

City magazines focus on your local metropolitan area and cover topics ranging from local restaurant reviews to the best places to find shopping bargains. They frequently have guest articles written on a variety of topics. State magazines have a broader focus, highlighting items of interest from across your state. Due to sometimes limited resources, these magazines often are open to guest columns that are submitted to them for consideration. As the name indicates, national magazines have a significantly broader focus and attempt to cover issues that appeal to readers all over the country. Although the competition to have a guest article included in a national magazine is fierce, use the same principles we discussed in contacting your local editors. Whether a publication is published locally, state-wide, or nationally, the editors all want to provide their readers with timely and relevant information.

MEDIA ACTION POINTS

Here are some tips on how to break into magazines:

✔ Contact editors and personal finance reporters and offer to be a source they call on when they're writing financial stories.

✔ Let editors know that you have clients who can be interviewed for stories, to give readers a real-life perspective. Note: If they interview your clients, you will be included as part of the interview.

✔ Approach editors about submitting a guest article for the magazine to print. Use the same approach as with newspapers.

GETTING INTO CYBERSPACE

Like newspapers, the Internet is packed with sites that update information on a daily basis. Reporters and writers for business and financial Internet sites also are always looking for expert commentary to provide perspective on the day's news events. The biggest benefit to being quoted as a financial expert on an Internet site is that it lends immediate national credibility to you. Another benefit of being interviewed for a business story on the Internet is that these web sites often keep feature articles on their site for several days, or even weeks, providing you with additional free media exposure. After being quoted, consider placing a link from your web site to that article. Then, when people visit your web site, it's easy for them to see that you are a recognized financial expert. These are good opportunities to build your credibility further.

COMPLIANCE

As you prepare your articles to send to the media, be sure to have the information approved through your compliance department, if necessary. Sometimes a review process may take several weeks, so plan your time accordingly. Remember, be sure to verify all numbers and statistics in your article before submitting them to the media because investment product limitations and tax laws may change frequently. This way, you're providing up-to-date information for your audience.

MEDIA ACTION POINTS

Here are the best ways to approach financial Internet sites:

✔ Contact editors and personal finance reporters and offer to be a source they call on when they're writing financial stories.

✔ Let personal finance reporters know that you have clients who can be interviewed for stories so they can get a real-life investor perspective.

✔ Regularly send them news story ideas that you feel their readers would be interested in, and offer to provide financial commentary.

GETTING YOUR OWN RADIO SHOW

Financial professionals often tell me that they want to have their own radio program. They want to be the financial guru sitting behind the microphone as thousands of people listen and call in with questions. Not only can this generate tremendous exposure for you and your business, but it's also a great way for people to get to know your personality, your investment philosophy, and how you work with clients. Then when they meet you in person, they feel as if they already know you. Most financial radio programs, for example, run for one to two hours on the weekend, when people generally are relaxed and outside of their work environment.

When you first begin hosting a radio program, it can be a bit unnerving to answer listener questions, since you never know what's coming at you next. However, the longer you do the program, the more comfortable you'll become answering almost any question that's posed. Plus, you'll have your notes in front of you to reference if you need them.

How do you talk your way into having your own radio program? The most common way is purchase a large block of advertising on the station. As part of your agreement, you can have your own radio show for the duration of your advertising contract. Most financial professionals you hear on local radio are paying the radio station a hefty sum each month for the privilege of presenting their program. The size of your local market typically determines the cost to advertise. For a two-hour radio program that runs on Saturday or Sunday, the fee may be $5,000 to $10,000 per month on average.

Here's how a paid radio program works:

- You pay a monthly advertising fee for the opportunity to have your own radio show.
- You negotiate with the station on the day and time of your show, the number and length of commercials the station will provide for your show, and the length of your contract.
- You determine the format of the show—the name of the program, what you talk about, and how your segment flows.

Whether you do a radio program depends on your financial commitment to this type of marketing. To help defray the cost of a radio show, you can:

- Have the wholesalers whose products you use commit to pay part of the cost each month.
- Have financial firms advertise during your program.
- Interview special guests from different financial companies and in return have them help with the show expenses.

Well-crafted radio shows can be very profitable for the financial professionals who host them. As with any type of marketing, the longer you have your own radio show, the more you will build up visibility and credibility. The beauty of radio is that you're not forced to speak only in two- to three-sentence sound bytes. Instead, you get to paint a full picture of how you work with clients, and people get to know you.

MEDIA ACTION POINTS

Here are five steps to selecting the radio station that is best for you:

1. Determine who your ideal client is.
2. Find out which are the top AM radio stations in your area. People don't generally listen to FM stations for news.
3. Have each station send you a demographic report showing you a description of who listens to the station. Compare the demographic reports with your ideal client demographics.
4. Choose between the station that is the most popular and the one that has the most listeners who fit your ideal client profile.
5. Negotiate every detail of your agreement. Radio stations have a rate card listing advertising rates. The station's representative will present it to you as if the rates are set in stone. However, don't settle for that. Remember: All media rates are highly negotiable.

CHALLENGE

View yourself as a marketing company that just happens to be in the financial services business. Adopt that mind-set and you will be wildly successful in your career. Financial professionals who take an organized and aggressive approach to their marketing initiatives reap big benefits by attracting more new clients and making the money they've always wanted. Once you start implementing these hard-hitting strategies, you can begin creating the kind of business you've always wanted.

CHAPTER FOUR

◆

BE THE EXPERT

Your phone rings. It's a reporter from your local newspaper, wanting you to comment on a breaking financial story. Finally your opportunity has arrived. But before you even have time to think, the reporter begins asking you questions. You answer as best you can, and five minutes later the interview is over.

Welcome to today's fast-paced media frenzy, where reporters and producers constantly are racing to meet deadlines. For you to succeed in this world, you must be prepared, flexible, and able to respond to the media's demands very quickly.

As the saying goes, you only get one chance to make a first impression. So preparing for your interview in advance is critical to your early success. Whether in television, radio, or print, there are two primary types of interviews: planned and spontaneous. Planned interviews include a television appearance or an interview on a radio station. In a spontaneous interview, a newspaper reporter might call you to comment on a story or a writer may want your opinion for a financial web site—all without any warning. Regardless of the type of interview you're doing, it pays to be prepared. How do you get prepared for an interview if you've never done one before? The strategy varies depending on whether you're preparing for television, radio, or print.

THE TELEVISION INTERVIEW

A television interview always falls into the "planned" category, although the amount of time you have to prepare will vary. For your first appearance, likely you will be given a few days' notice. Occasionally, if you have an ongoing relationship with a station, you may receive only a few hours' notice if there's a breaking financial story. In either case, when you are contacted initially, ask the producer these following questions:

- What is the topic?
- Who is the audience? Who are the typical viewers of the program?
- What are the key points you'd like me to get across to the audience?

Once you have answers to these questions, your next step is to watch or listen to the program, so you can familiarize yourself with the anchor or interviewer's style, the format of the program, and the set where you'll be interviewed.

On television, what you see is what you get. It's important for you to feel comfortable and confident before the interview. The best way to prepare is to practice being interviewed. Before my first television appearance, I had my wife ask me sample questions and I practiced answering the questions in different ways. Then I sat in front of a mirror and practiced talking so I could see what I would look like to viewers. Talking to yourself can be a bit uncomfortable at first, but it's a great way to observe how you speak and gesture.

Another skill you should practice is answering questions in short "sound bytes." News interviews often last only five to eight seconds. If taped in advance, the interview actually may have taken 10 to 15 minutes. However, producers don't want someone who drones on. You need short, snappy responses that deliver the information in easy-to-understand and memorable ways. If your interview isn't live, expect it to be edited down to only a few sentences. The key is to make those few sentences catchy and insightful.

As you prepare, consider sitting the way you'll most likely be sitting during the interview. On TV, you'll typically be at a news desk with a camera pointed directly at you that you'll talk into, or you may be sitting on a couch or chair talking to the anchor, who is sitting in a chair at an angle to you. If you're sitting on a couch, you won't be looking into the camera—your eye focus will be on the anchor. It's important to be comfortable with where you'll be sitting and where your eye focus should be. If you're not looking where you should, the audience will be able to tell that something is "off." You also may want to familiarize yourself with the equipment you'll be using. You'll probably be wearing a lapel microphone and possibly an earpiece so that you'll know when you're about to be interviewed and can hear the news anchor speaking to you. One way to prepare in advance that I've found helpful is to sit down and mentally walk through every aspect of the interview.

Ten Steps to a Successful Interview

1. Arrive at the studio early, and be friendly to the security guard.

2. Greet the producer with a firm handshake and a big smile and tell her how happy you are to be there.

3. Sit in the green room (the name for the waiting area for guests).

4. Walk onto the set, smile, and say "hi" to the camera people.

5. When it's time for the interview, picture yourself talking just to the host or, if it will make you more comfortable, envision yourself speaking to a client.

6. Give a great answer to each question.

7. At the end of your interview, the producer walks up to you and says "Great job!"

8. When you leave, tell the anchors and producers it was great to meet them.

9. Ask the producer how she felt the interview went (to hear it in her words).

10. Ask her to please call you again.

Your goal should be to run through this interview so many times mentally that by the time you get there, you feel comfortable in your new surroundings. By visualizing every step of the interview in advance, you'll boost your confidence and be more prepared. As you visualize, do it realistically. What if something goes wrong or if you are asked an unexpected question in the interview? How will you handle that? Practicing some worst-case scenarios in your mind can better prepare you for any curveball that might be thrown your way.

Practice this visualization at least once a day until the day of your interview. Then, as you're driving to the studio, utilize that time again to picture how you'll answer the questions posed to you. Use that drive time to imagine doing a flawless and interesting interview and being congratulated on a job well done by the producer. I strongly believe that if you first envision success in your mind, you are far more likely to achieve it in reality.

MEDIA ACTION POINTS

- ✔ When you're contacted about a television interview, ask about the topic, audience, and key points the producer wants you to cover.
- ✔ Practice being interviewed.
- ✔ Visualize the interview ahead of time.

THE RADIO INTERVIEW

Although you're not seen on the radio, it's just as important that you're prepared for an appearance. In fact, because you won't have the advantage of using gestures and facial expressions to convey your message, you may need to prepare even more to ensure that your voice communicates well. Have someone ask you questions, and respond in short sentences. Keep in mind that when you appear on the radio, it's all about painting a picture for the audience using only words. Financial topics can be complicated. Those financial experts who can explain complex topics in a manner that makes sense will do well in radio.

Just as with a television interview, ask the producer about the topic you'll be speaking on, the audience, and the message they want you to get across. Keep the answers to those questions in mind as you practice. As you prepare, use the visualization techniques I described earlier. Picture yourself responding well to the questions, speaking articulately and with an authoritative voice, and imagine the program director congratulating you and asking you to come back.

It is also important to be prepared for the radio station environment. When you're interviewed on the radio, typically you'll be wearing headphones so you can hear the person interviewing you. Sometimes you'll be in the same room as the interviewer; other times you may be in an adjoining room. The key is to talk to the person just as if you were carrying on a normal conversation. If you aren't in the same room with the interviewer, try to imagine that you are talking to someone so that your interview comes across as conversational in tone.

MEDIA ACTION POINTS

✔ Practice your speaking skills for a radio interview.

✔ Visualize yourself speaking well and articulately.

✔ Be prepared for the environment.

THE PRINT INTERVIEW

Most newspaper or print interviews will be spontaneous. Between two and four o'clock in the afternoon, most reporters are completing stories for afternoon deadlines. A reporter or writer may call you, thanks to the faxes or e-mails you've sent, and want you to comment on a story he or she is writing. Generally it is more difficult to prepare for this type of interview, but you can be as prepared as possible by following a few simple steps.

First, stay up-to-date on what's going on in the financial world. Make it a point to read a little every day, whether it's the newspaper, magazines, or a financial web site.

MEDIA ACTION POINTS

Some web sites you can refer to include:

bloomberg.com

cnbc.com

cnn.com

foxnews.com

money.cnn.com

msn.com

msnbc.com

Each web site updates its business and financial news 24 hours a day so you can stay updated on what is happening—and all in just minutes. The key is to stay current on what is going on. One of the nice benefits of being "in the know" is that it allows you as a financial advisor to be able to speak more knowledgeably to your clients and prospective clients. If you're able to sprinkle into your discussion information about how an upcoming economic report may be of interest to your clients, they will feel that you know what is going on.

Keep in mind the purpose behind staying up-to-date on the financial world; I'm not talking about reading up on the world of financial advisors, or how to improve your practice, sell more products, or market yourself. I'm talking about reading about the topics that the average person wants to know about—the economy, the market, how to save for college and retirement, the latest home mortgage rates, and so on. Use your reading time to become an expert on the topics people are interested in, not the topics yourself are most interested in.

Next, when you do begin your interview, stay focused. Remember that you've been waiting for this opportunity, and now it's your time to shine. When a reporter or writer calls you, stop everything else that you're doing. Don't check e-mails or sift through paper in the background—doing so will make you appear to be distracted. Give the reporter your undivided attention. Listen intently to what the reporter is asking you. In that moment, envision yourself as a reader of the article when it comes out in tomorrow's newspaper. What could you say that might capture the reader's interest? What is a key issue that your ideal clients are concerned about that you could incorporate into your answer? Keep those things in mind as you respond.

More than any other media outlet, the newspaper demands that you use short phrases. Practice wording your answers exactly as you want them to appear in the newspaper. By speaking slowly and succinctly to reporters, you will increase the odds of being quoted correctly or even being quoted at all. One secret to conducting a great newspaper interview is to ask the reporter what the angle of the story is—the key message that he or she wants to communicate to readers. Asking this question shows the reporter that you are seriously interested in helping with the story.

When talking to a newspaper reporter, remember that what you say is going to be written down. The more you say, the more difficult it is to accurately capture exactly what you said, which can lead to being misquoted. Here's a good rule of thumb to follow: Speak in one to two sentence sound bytes to the reporter. Trust me, this isn't easy. It seems as if most financial professionals are somehow engineered to explain things in a long, drawn-out way, perhaps thinking that makes us sound more intelligent. Remember that, many times, the reporter knows very little about the financial world. It's important for you to speak clearly and briefly so the reporter can record accurately the essence of what you want to communicate.

Another great way to prepare ahead of time for a print interview is to read other financial experts' quotes in the newspaper or in articles posted on the Internet. You'll find that these quoted experts have three common characteristics.

1. They sound catchy. Good interviewees are able to toss in buzzwords or key phrases in their interviews.

2. They quickly encapsulate a key message in one or two sentences. They have learned to say very succinctly something that the average financial professional would need a paragraph or more to explain.

3. They manage to make a point without predicting the future. They use their words carefully to make a statement while not guaranteeing what will happen.

HOW TO WOW THE MEDIA

When a reporter calls, you have two options: You can begin to answer the questions right away, assuming you have the information you need in front of you or in your existing knowledge base. Or you can politely say, "I definitely want to talk with you about this. However, you've caught me in the middle of something. Can I call you right back?" This is the buy-yourself-some-time strategy. Let's examine how this strategy works.

1. You've told the reporter that you're definitely interested in speaking with her.

2. You've said that even though you are very busy, you will take the time to speak with her. This conveys to the reporter that she is important.

3. You've put yourself in the best position to think through how you might answer her questions so you can be well prepared for the real interview. Take a few minutes and think through how you might answer the questions, or look up any information you need and call the reporter right back. Reporters on deadlines will appreciate your quick follow-up.

For you to become a regular source for the media, you have to be available and accessible. Tell your staff that if you receive a call from the media, someone should either come get you immediately or tell the media contact that you definitely want to talk with him or her and you'll call right back. When reporters call, they are not surprised if you're busy. But they generally want to talk to you within an hour of calling. Call them back from your car or before your next appointment. If you're doing a phone interview when your next clients arrive, have your receptionist say you will be with them in a few minutes because you're doing an interview with X media. Doing this allows you to leverage the media to increase your credibility with your clients, which should be one of your main goals. Most clients are understanding of the delay and impressed that their financial professional is the expert the media calls on for insight.

If you call your media contact back and get voice mail, say you are returning her call and would be happy to speak with her. If you don't hear back from her right away, keep calling the contact back until you reach her, don't just leave a message. Reporters and producers will appreciate your persistence in getting back in touch with them. Doing so will virtually guarantee that you will be one of the people who gets quoted in their stories. As you speak with reporters, remember that typically they use two to four sources per story. You want to stand out. Be upbeat and speak succinctly to help ensure that you'll not only be quoted but also quoted accurately.

MEDIA ACTION POINTS

✔ To prepare for a print interview, stay up-to-date on what's going on in the financial world by reading every day.

✔ When a reporter calls, if you need to buy time, let her know that you're interested in talking to her but you're in the middle of something and will call her right back.

✔ When you're being interviewed, focus 100 percent on the reporter's questions. Think about what readers would want to know.

✔ Practice answering questions in succinct sound bytes.

HOW TO SPEAK TO THE MEDIA

It's critical to remember that when you're speaking to the media, you must try to say the right things carefully and deliberately. Once a word comes out of your mouth, it can't be taken back. For good or bad, anything that is said can be used for you or against you. Now that I've scared you into never speaking to the media, let me put things in the proper perspective. At some point, everyone who works with the media says something or answers a question in a way that he sometimes wishes he could take back. We're all human, so it's going to happen. The key is learn from your mistakes. Over time you will begin to think quickly enough to avoid most of the potholes that wait on the road to media success.

How do you speak to the media in a way that the audience wants and still accurately paint a true picture of who you are? The first step is to begin to listen carefully and watch guests being interviewed, and study them. What do they say? How do they answer questions? Eventually, you'll begin to quickly notice which guests are really interesting and hold your attention and which ones seem to drone on and on until you wonder when they'll stop talking.

MEDIA ACTION POINTS

Successful guests exhibit seven traits:

1. They smile when the anchor introduces them.
2. They answer questions without skipping a beat.
3. They answer questions in three- to five-sentence responses.
4. They look directly into the camera or right at the anchor (whichever is appropriate).
5. They dress for the occasion—professional and sharp.
6. They don't talk too fast.
7. They appear confident and likable.

By observing these success traits and incorporating them into your interviews, you can become a repeat guest on your local news programs. But you also need to avoid making the mistakes made by some unsuccessful guests. We've all seen it. You're watching the news and you begin to cringe as you realize that the "expert" doesn't communicate very well. As this guest gets tongue-tied and appears to be rambling, he quickly loses credibility and respect. He may be very knowledgeable, but you and the rest of the audience will judge him by how poorly he communicates.

To truly leverage the media for success, it's not enough simply to appear on television or in the newspaper. The key is to communicate in a way that makes sense to people and makes you stand out as someone who is highly knowledgeable. If you can accomplish this, people not only will listen to what you say, but they also will begin to look forward to hearing or reading what you say. When you reach that point, you have been transformed in people's minds from someone who just appears in the media to a trusted advisor.

Remember this key point: How you speak matters. Some of the most intelligent people are not called on by the media because they aren't able to communicate effectively or understandably. Overcomplicating things only confuses people more. Here are some surefire ways to know if you're communicating effectively:

- Your clients tell you that they like the way you explain things to them.
- When you appear on television or radio, people at the station tell you that they appreciate the way you keep your explanations simple.
- People who watch you or read your quotes tell you that you really make sense.

It is important to practice speaking well. Countless business studies have shown that a person's ability to speak and communicate effectively is one of the leading indicators of how successful a person is in all aspects of life. Although we each have a unique style of communicating, those financial professionals who understand their communication style and then leverage that style in the media have a great opportunity to achieve success.

MEDIA ACTION POINTS

Some ways to improve your speaking ability:

✔ Practice reading out loud. Emphasize different words, and listen to how it makes the same sentence sound different.

✔ Vary your speed as you read. Read some sentences a little faster, then slow down to emphasize key points.

✔ Vary your pitch as you read. Use higher and lower inflections to communicate your meaning.

✔ Say the alphabet and emphasize different letters each time.

The purpose of these exercises is to train yourself to speak authoritatively and confidently and to discover the importance of variation in your speech. If you speak too fast in an interview, you can appear nervous or "salesy." If you speak too slowly, you can come across as unfocused. That's why it's important for you to practice these methods so you can present yourself as a confident and knowledgeable communicator.

Remember, when you are invited to do an interview or make an appearance, the goal of the producer or reporter is not to put you on the spot and embarrass you. If you become flustered or embarrassed, not only will you look bad, but those interviewing you will look bad as well. When you're being interviewed as part of a news story, the media doesn't want you to have the deer-in-the-headlights look. For these reasons, it's important to communicate ahead of time with your producers about your topic and to use a script, if possible, which will help you avoid any awkward moments. Remember: The key to a good interview is to give a great answer to the first question. Doing so makes a good first impression and gives you confidence throughout the rest of the interview.

THINK ON YOUR FEET

One of the biggest concerns that advisors share with me is their fear about being asked a question they don't know anything about, or not being able to think of an answer quickly enough. To help you overcome these concerns, I want to review some techniques that I use if I don't know the exact answer to a question. First of all, you always should be as prepared as possible before an interview. However, there will be times when you "get stuck" answering a question during an interview, so you need to practice using "filler" words. Filler words are terms or phrases you can use as you are trying to think of what to say or when you absolutely have no idea how to answer the question you've been asked. At all costs, you want to avoid saying that you don't know the answer. Instead, you want to frame your response in such a way that you sound very intelligent, while only lightly touching on the answer.

Here are some examples of how to answer tricky questions during a television or radio interview.

If you're asked about a business/financial issue that you don't know the answer to, say:

> (Anchor name), that's an interesting question. An issue like this can be addressed from several different angles. Let me give you this perspective . . .

> *Explanation:* This approach lets you answer the question but in the way that you want to answer it. You should know at least something about the topic, so speak on what you know about it.

If you're asked a question and you want to convey a key message, say:

> This is a question I get asked frequently, and what I want our viewers to know is what this means to them . . .

> *Explanation:* This approach lets you answer the question in a way you think would be most interesting to the audience, even if it doesn't necessarily answer the anchor's question.

If you're asked about a report that you know nothing about, say:

> An economic report like this one is likely to give investors some indication about different conditions affecting the market. One thing that is interesting to point out about this report and other important economic data is that Wall Street is always wary of surprises. We'll have to keep an eye on how this report turns out, because that will determine how investors will respond to it.

If you're asked about a legal issue affecting the market, say:

> (Anchor name), while I'm not an attorney and not an expert on legal matters, issues like this can be very complex. Generally, when all is said and done, the focus of things like this goes back to doing the right thing for the average investor like you and me. So we'll have to watch how this case unfolds.

The first rule of appearing in the media is never to look surprised by questions that you're asked. As you become more comfortable doing interviews, you'll begin to realize that there is always something you can say that sounds intelligent. Although what you say may not necessarily answer the question directly, you still can come across as knowledgeable by calmly saying something relevant, then shifting the topic. As you work with the media, remember that *how* you say something is often more important than *what* you say. In emergency situations like the ones I have just described, it's best to answer the question coolly and continue. What's the secret to answering interview questions like a star? For every question you answer in the media, keep in mind this guiding principle: What does this mean to the average investor?

If you can learn to respond to that question consistently in every answer you give, you are likely to place yourself on the path to long-term media success. After all, that's what the media wants: someone who can take the seemingly complex financial issues of Wall Street and break them down in a way that makes sense to average people. These are the people who go to work every day to help support their families and who invest their hard-earned money in the stock market to help save for their kids' education and their retirement. Most people don't want to become financial experts; they simply want to understand what the financial lingo means to them and how it might impact their family. Think of yourself as the water filter of financial information. You take in all the complex financial news, but what comes out of you is clear and smooth financial information that provides viewers with what they need to know.

MEDIA ACTION POINTS

✔ If you're asked a question you don't know the answer to during an interview, use "filler" words.

✔ In your interviews, always answer the question: What does this mean to the average investor?

BE ONE OF THE SOURCES
THE MEDIA CALLS ON

It's important to understand a fundamental difference in how the print media (newspaper, Internet, magazines) and the television and radio media conduct interviews and whom they interview. Although TV and radio producers typically use only one source for their stories, print media reporters commonly use three to four sources for each story so they can get different perspectives for their readers. Reporters writing a national story may call on many advisors in different parts of the country. They may call a couple of independent advisors and then some stockbrokers and financial professionals who work for large firms. Or they may call an outside expert on a financial topic or a company analyst to provide perspective. The key is for you to be one of the three to four sources the reporter calls. Don't be greedy and think you should be the only financial professional the reporter interviews. It just doesn't work that way. What you want to do is work your way onto the reporter's short list of financial professionals and begin to stand out as a contact who always gives a great interview.

Think about when you buy a product or service. What companies stand out in your mind? Typically, they are the ones that deliver a great service or product at a great price. Normally what sticks out most in your mind is the level of personal service you receive. In today's society, even small things stand out to us because so many companies simply don't focus on their quality of service. Candidly, you are there to serve the media. If you have a constant attitude of "How can I best serve you?" you are setting yourself up for long-term success—not only in the media but in how you run your business overall.

LEARN TO
COMMUNICATE CAUTIOUSLY

One of the worst fears of company compliance departments is that their financial advisors will say the wrong things when they speak to the media. Because of that, most firms work closely with their advisors to ensure they know what to say and what not to say. As you begin working with the media, remember to work with your compliance department. It's there to help. They want you to succeed and want to help keep you out of trouble.

Remember as you're talking to the media to use hedge words such as "consider," "possible," "potential," and "opportunity." Never allow yourself to be perceived as giving direct advice to people through the media. However, you can dole out great investment strategies for them to "consider" and "review" and "see if it might benefit their situation." Mentally picture yourself as a doctor who can diagnose people's financial problems only after thoroughly "examining" them. When you see a doctor for a particular problem, she typically doesn't rush in and immediately prescribe a medication or treatment for you. Normally, she looks at your file, asks questions, examines you, and then prescribes a suitable solution. Keep in mind that you cannot adequately diagnose someone's financial problems until you have met with that person and carefully evaluated his situation.

Media outlets want timely information for viewers or readers. In interviews, often you will be asked about the stock market and individual companies, and you may even be asked to give your predictions about future performance on Wall Street. Obviously, you're not a fortune-teller, or you wouldn't be reading this book. How do you answer these difficult questions? Your goal in appearing in the media is to build credibility for yourself. If you're doling out predictions as you talk with the media, you're indicating that you know the future, and that's bound to get you into trouble. Instead, aim to give the key information that the media outlet wants, but not to present yourself as a stock market soothsayer. If you make predictions about the market, you're bound to be wrong at some point. And when you're wrong, you'll be chipping away at your credibility instead of building it up. It's best to stay out of the prediction game.

As you talk to reporters and get interviewed on the radio and television, your goal should be to communicate in a very intelligent and relevant way and to avoid making any predictions regarding what might happen to the stock market, a given company, or an individual stock. Here's the bad news: You'll get asked about these things all the time. The best thing you can do is to be prepared. The key is to answer your questions in such a way that you come across as highly credible, without giving any specifics. It's a fine line to walk. How do you do that?

Here are some examples of good ways and bad ways to handle questions:

Question:	How do you think the stock market will end up by the end of the year?
Bad Answer:	Given the fact that the market is currently at (x), my prediction would be that it would hit (y) by the end of the year. I think you're going to see sectors X, Y, and Z do really well and you're going to see some trouble for companies A, B, and C. I can confidently say that this will be a great year for all investors.
Good Answer:	(Anchor name), I certainly don't have a crystal ball and would love to meet someone who does. But I can tell you this. How the stock market finishes this year will depend on several factors, such as company earnings, the overall health of the economy and how comfortable average investors like you and me feel spending our hard-earned dollars. It really depends on how Wall Street responds to how it feels the economy is doing.
Question:	What are the hot stocks that investors should buy right now?

Bad Answer:　　I think the hot stocks right now are companies D, E, and F. Their products are solid and they are selling a lot right now. I don't think anyone could go wrong with these stocks. It's a no-lose deal.

Good Answer:　　In my experience, I've found that if one stock is hot today, then it can turn cold tomorrow just as fast. So here's what I tell my clients—invest based on your personal risk tolerance and your time-frame for your goals. If you're a young investor with 30 years until retirement, you may be able to take a higher level of risk and be more aggressive with your investments.

Question:　　If someone had a windfall of $50,000 today, where would you tell them to invest it?

Bad Answer:　　Well, I'll tell you what I would do. I would put half into Company A or Tech Mutual Fund B. And here's why. They're really low right now and I think they're going to go up in value. Things like this can move fast so I would invest in it right away.

Good Answer:　　Here's what I would suggest the person do. First, ask yourself this important question: "Where would $50,000 do me and my family the most good right now and in the future?" Then write down on a sheet of paper all of your options. That list might include paying off high-interest debt, starting your kids' education accounts, or investing money for retirement. Everyone's situation is different, so work closely with a financial advisor to see what options may be best for you.

As you speak with the media, it's important to focus on what you're saying and how it may come across. Although it may be tempting to give your personal opinion on a particular stock or issue, remember that you want to be objective and provide factual commentary while not directly telling people what to do. After all, the goal is not to set yourself up as someone who has insider information. You also don't want to make a prediction that turns out to be dead wrong; if you do, you'll end up looking very badly and you'll lose credibility. Instead, you want to come across as someone who is very knowledgeable and trustworthy. That's the kind of guest media outlets want to interview on a regular basis.

STAY IN FRONT OF THE MEDIA

One of the biggest complaints I hear from advisors who have been in the media before is that they were never called again to do another interview. My response is to ask them what they have done to get back in touch with the media—to let them know they are still around. Most advisors admit they have done nothing to reinitiate that relationship. In order for you to appear consistently in the media, it's critical to remember this point: Because the media are always in motion, you need to contact them continually.

As I discussed earlier, the key to building your visibility in the media is to appear on a frequent basis. In television and radio, the critical step is positioning yourself to be invited back. How do you do that?

First of all, you must be a team player. Just because you're the expert the media called on doesn't mean that you're now a step above everyone else. Once you set foot into a newsroom or are about to be interviewed, your purpose is to help the producers and anchors do their job by creating the best segment possible. Offer ideas on topics that will interest the audience or possible questions that will allow you to give great answers that will make sense to the audience. Your producers may not rely on you much at first, but the more often you appear, the more they will depend on you to help improve their stories and interviews.

Another way to get invited back is to be upbeat during the interview and excited to be there. No anchor or reporter wants to interview someone who's a dud. They want people who are energetic and happy to be part of the interview. Good guests make the anchors even better because when the anchor and guest are really clicking, the audience picks up on the fact that they work well together. Media outlets want people who are in sync with their anchors and reporters because it makes their newscasts look more polished.

The next way to get invited back is to treat everyone with whom you come into contact like kings and queens—from the security guard who lets you in the building to the reporter who calls you on the phone. Put your manners into high gear. Media newsrooms can be fast-paced, and most media people are overworked and underpaid. Anyone who is kind to them is not only deeply appreciated, but really stands out. When you go onto the set, be extremely nice and interactive with the anchors and remember their names. The final way to get invited back is to know your stuff. When the camera light turns on or the *on air* sign lights up at the radio station, it's time to give it all you've got.

MEDIA ACTION POINTS

✔ Make it your goal to be one of the sources the media calls on for their stories.

✔ Avoid coming across as a "stock-market fortune-teller."

✔ Proactively seek out ways to get invited back for more interview opportunities.

NEWSROOM ETIQUETTE

When you go to a television or radio studio for an interview, stay out of the way and do exactly what you're told. Remember, you'll be one of many guests who will appear on the show that day.

Be on time. Typically you should arrive at the studio 30 to 60 minutes before your scheduled interview time, although this will vary with different media outlets. This amount of time allows you to get settled, meet with your producer, review your questions, and prepare for your interview. It also assures the producer that you're there and ready.

Be prepared for the possibility that the producer may ask for your help in drafting your interview questions, even if you're not using a prewritten script you've already seen. Be sure to ask what key messages the producer wants you to get across in your interview. This will help you stand out because people rarely ask this question.

Many interviewees are interested only in getting their own message across, a message that is usually "Buy what I'm selling." Once the producer tells you what she is looking for, then you can help brainstorm questions for the interview.

Because each media outlet's goal is to keep its audience informed of breaking news, there is always the possibility that your interview may be postponed or canceled altogether. Although news programs are scripted in advance, if an important local or national news item occurs, expect the media outlet to shift its focus to that right away in order to stay ahead of the competition. If that happens, they might tell you to be on standby: if they can squeeze you in, they will. Or it's possible that they may tell you that your interview has been canceled. If that does happen, do not be upset or act annoyed or inconvenienced. Instead, say "No problem. I'm a team player. You've got to do what's best for the team. I completely understand. When can we reschedule the interview?" That's the attitude the media wants—helpful, understanding, and flexible. Remember that no producer likes to tell a guest that his segment has been canceled, but a producer's first commitment is to the news.

MEDIA ACTION POINTS

✔ Arrive at the studio 30 to 60 minutes early for a television or radio interview.

✔ Be prepared to help draft your questions if you're not using a prewritten script.

✔ If your segment is canceled, be gracious and offer to reschedule.

✔ Be a team player when you work with producers, anchors, and other media people.

LOOK LIKE THE EXPERT

When you go to the doctor, you expect to see someone dressed in a lab coat or in scrubs, right? What if the doctor walked into the room where you were waiting wearing shorts, a T-shirt, and sneakers? My first reaction would be to get out of there as quickly as I could. However, if I did stay, I would have a lingering concern in my mind, wondering why this doctor was dressed this way. I would have less respect for him and probably question his remarks more than usual.

This same analogy holds true with how financial professionals dress. In my consultations with financial advisors across the country, I am always amazed to see the casual attire many wear to the office. How do people expect a financial advisor to dress? I believe that the default dress for all financial professionals is a long-sleeve shirt and tie or a dress shirt and sport coat for men, and a business suit or blouse and skirt/slacks for women. People expect this business attire. It's all about first impressions.

From a consumer standpoint, there is no downside to dressing in business attire. Financial professionals sometimes rationalize that people don't really care how advisors dress; they care only how much their advisors know about financial planning. I strongly disagree. I believe you always should dress for a big opportunity.

What does dressing well have to do with the media? In the media, appearance is extremely important. To be judged as a professional, you have to dress well. You will be judged not only by what you say, but also by how you look and dress, and your image will play a big role in establishing yourself as a financial expert. If you were watching television and the news anchor said, "We're now joined by financial expert Joe Smith," and Joe Smith appears on camera in a short-sleeve golf shirt, you're going to wonder why Joe doesn't have on a coat and tie. Why will you think this? Because the general perception is that lawyers, bankers, and financial people dress professionally.

Your image can make or break you in terms of your media success. When you appear in the media, you're reinforcing your image—good or bad. In the media, every day is a day both to make a great first impression and to further build your credibility with your existing audience. As time passes, you will begin to attract the very investors you want to work with, because they will understand and appreciate your approach to investing and financial planning. Prior to coming to your office, those investors will be wondering if the nicely dressed, professional-looking financial expert they see in the media will be the same one they meet in person. When potential clients realize that those two personalities are indeed the same person, they are more likely to do business with you.

Achieving success as a financial professional is all about predicting what your potential clients expect and then meeting and exceeding those expectations. Don't rationalize yourself out of potential business simply because you'd rather come to the office in jeans. When people meet with a financial advisor, they expect the person to look successful, to have a nice office, and to communicate well. When they realize that one of those expectations is not being met, it might not necessarily be a deal-breaker, but it could place a small seed of doubt in their mind about whether this particular financial advisor is right for them. If you don't look professional, then throughout your presentation, potential clients will be slightly distracted, wondering if they can overlook this seemingly small infraction. Here's the bottom line: If people expect you to have a certain appearance as a financial advisor, then deliver on that expectation. Don't try to change it.

As I work with advisors to help them attract their ideal clients, one of the things on their wish list is to attract more retired people as clients. Generally retirees have more money and are more profitable to work with, so it makes good business sense to target this group of prospective clients. I have found that the older clients I work with tend to dress up for our meetings. You see, many older clients believe that dressing well is a sign of respect toward the person with whom they're meeting. And sometimes they will comment on how well I dress. On days when I have a big meeting with an existing or a prospective client, I intentionally hang my suit coat on the door behind me. Doing this conveys a subtle message that we're there to take care of business. Dressing too casually sends the subtle message that you're not a professional, and retired clients may view you as "too casual" for their taste.

When you appear on television, the audience has the perception that you were selected to be there because you're knowledgeable and an expert on your topic. That's the image you want to maintain each and every time you appear. Let me share with you some steps that I follow to dress well for the media.

MEDIA ACTION POINTS

✔ Study different news anchors and how they dress. Often, they have a clothing allowance because they have to dress well. Try to mimic them.

✔ Things look differently on TV from how they look face-to-face. Select clothing combinations that look well together and will come across well on camera.

✔ Have someone who dresses well help you select what to wear.

✔ Keep a small notepad and write down what you wear each time you appear, so you don't duplicate the same outfit with each interview.

I have found that dressing well lays the foundation for success. Producers and viewers simply relate better to people who dress well, and the professional demeanor comes across better to their audience. What a powerful and rare combination it is to find someone who dresses well and can communicate the topic in a way that really makes sense with the audience! Those are two of the key ingredients to tasting success in the media. Then you'll be the financial expect your prospective clients expect to see when they arrive at your office.

TRAIN YOUR CLIENTS TO KEEP THEIR MONEY WITH YOU

Other financial professionals are targeting the wealthy investors you want to reach on a weekly basis. When they open their mailbox, often they receive more invitations to free dinner seminars than credit card offers. My clients have told me that sometimes they receive one to two investment advisor solicitations per week. This aggressive marketing on the part of the financial community means that your best clients are continually being wooed away to another firm. How can you launch a successful counterattack and not only protect and keep your existing clients but begin securing new clients?

The key is communication, communication, communication. People like to be kept in touch with, met with, and mailed to. They want to know that you are on top of their accounts and monitoring things on their behalf. Clients want to feel confident that their advisor is caring for their investments. If clients feel that their advisor has their best interests at heart and is communicating on a frequent basis, that advisor will not only have a happier, less worried client base, but also will attract new clients whose advisors simply don't call them anymore. Because of the vastness of the media outlets, using them effectively is a powerful way to make yourself stand out as the financial expert people can trust.

Once you realize that your clients are being marketed to aggressively, it's time for you to go on the offensive. How do you do that? The first step is to bring it up with your clients in your meetings. Here's what I say to each of my clients during our review meetings: "Richard and Mary, if you don't mind me asking, how many mailings or phone calls do you receive each week from other financial companies?" (Pause for their answer.) "That's what I thought. What has happened is that you are most likely on a mailing list of high-net-worth people. Today there is no shortage of financial professionals out there. All of them are trying to pitch something bigger and better to get people to invest with them. At some point, you probably will get something in the mail or have someone call you with a product that may sound too good to be true. Or you may be tempted to go to a dinner seminar just to see if something can really be that good. Here's what I'd like you to do. Whenever you hear about something that sounds incredibly good, before you do anything, call me first and let's talk about it. I try to stay on top of things, but occasionally something new comes out. I can take a look at it for you and help you determine whether it's a good solution for you or not."

By saying this to your clients, you're accomplishing three things:

1. You've shed light on the issue that your clients are being prospected by other financial professionals.
2. You've openly acknowledged that your clients may be tempted to take a closer look at what another financial professional has to offer. If your clients have felt this way, they are relieved now that it is out in the open.

3. You have solidified your position as their financial professional of choice and affirmed that your clients should consult you before making investment decisions, so you can offer them direction.

If you have this conversation on a regular basis with your clients, you will help to build some insulation around your long-term relationships with them.

MORE MEDIA FOR YOU EQUALS LESS WORRY FOR YOUR CLIENTS

We're faced with purchasing decisions every day. After each decision you make, it's natural to evaluate whether you did the right thing, whether you've purchased a tangible product or an intangible relationship with a financial professional. That's what your clients deal with all the time. But consider how reassuring it is for them to see their financial advisor on television or see him quoted in the newspaper. They'll think that their financial advisor also was selected by the news media as *their* financial expert. Then they're able to tell their colleagues that they work with the advisor on Channel X or who is frequently quoted in such-and-such a newspaper.

Throughout history, the stock market has experienced periods when it has been down for several years at a time. Times like those can be very difficult for clients and can seriously strain the advisor-client relationship. It's only human nature for clients to begin to worry when things aren't going well and when there is so much uncertainty in the stock market. At times of such volatility, people begin seriously considering taking their investments to extremes. Some might think about moving all their money from the stock market and tying it up in five-year CDs. The pendulum can swing quickly in terms of how people think and feel about their investments.

In my experience, the simple fact that I was appearing in the media so often helped put my clients at ease. My appearances helped me reassure my existing clients and also attract many new clients whose advisors had stopped communicating with them. Whether it's with existing clients or someone else's clients, make communication your top priority. In my current client review meetings, people often say that just seeing me on TV made them feel better. Even during times of extreme market volatility, they knew that I was a constant in their lives because I hadn't disappeared. Instead, I used times of economic uncertainty to create more media opportunities for myself so that clients and prospective clients could see me even more often. This is a great example of how you can plant the seeds and cultivate profitable long-term financial planning relationships through the media.

THE MEDIA CAN HELP GROW YOUR BUSINESS

Your appearances in the media can not only help confirm in your clients' minds that they made the right choice; they also can help you gain exactly the clients you want to work with. The key is to tailor your message so that it appeals to the exact people you want to reach. Because often you may be asked about a specific economic report or company, your focus can't always be on how you work with clients. But this relationship is what viewers like to hear about most, because that's what they want to know. After all, they are concerned about these very issues—investing with less risk, having more income in retirement, and knowing all the investment options available to them so they can make more informed decisions. The more you work in the media, the more comfortable you'll get answering questions like these. The key is to answer the real question, which is "What does this mean to the average investor?" By constantly keeping that perspective in mind when you're interviewed, you'll grow into the role of the financial expert whom people will begin to trust.

Let's talk about other ways you can answer questions that will make people listen to what you're saying. Remember, the first step is to determine whom you would like to work with—your ideal client. Regardless of what media outlets you appear in, you want to position yourself in that outlet to attract the clients you want. As people see or read you over a long period of time, you can cultivate that attention so that they'll want to work with you as their financial advisor.

Here are some key phrases you can say that will appeal to specific target markets. These kinds of phrases would work for all aspects of the media. I call it the "what/that" model.

- "What this (name the issue) means to retired investors is that (describe a benefit in a few words)."

- "What this (name the issue) means to parents saving for their kids' education is that (describe a benefit in a few words)."

- "What this (name the issue) means to the beginning investor is that (describe a benefit in a few words)."

- "What this (name the issue) means to a widowed investor is that (describe a benefit in a few words)."

- "What this (name the issue) means to a divorced investor is that (describe a benefit in a few words)."

- "What this (name the issue) means to a single investor is that (describe a benefit in a few words)."

The goal is to pick an issue that your target market is concerned about and talk about it. Following the model I've laid out for you lets you create a sound byte that the audience or reader can understand easily. Plus, when you're being interviewed by a newspaper reporter, what you've said is short enough to get quoted correctly. Reporters can understand a short response. Remember that on the other end of the phone line, a reporter is feverishly writing down what you just said so she can go back and use one or two key phrases for her actual article. Your aim is to spoon-feed her the key phrases right off the bat. By deliberately speaking in key phrases, you are almost guaranteed to be quoted exactly. Believe me, reporters like to have things made easier for them. And the more you speak to reporters, the better you become at naturally speaking in short, catchy sentences. It just takes practice. And the more times you do it, your confidence will build as your name appears in the media for all to see.

THE "WOW" FACTOR

When you begin appearing in the media on a regular basis, people will begin to perceive that you are very busy—perhaps even too busy for them. How do you get around that? Whenever I appear on television or am quoted in the newspaper, I try to celebrate by calling my top clients. Let's say I just appeared on the morning news. When I get back to my office, I call a few of my top clients to touch base, give them an update on their accounts, and say, "I was thinking about you and wanted to give you a call." Odds are that some of them just saw me on TV. Now they're confused as to how I could have just been on TV and yet still have thought of them.

The goal is to utilize the media to overwhelm your clients with surprisingly great service. That's how the "wow" factor works. Consistently do the things they've always hoped a skilled financial professional would do for them—the follow-up, the calling, the face-to-face meetings—and envelop them with personal service. So many advisors overlook the small things in their relationships with their clients that when financial professionals simply do what they say they're going to do, it tends to exceed many people's expectations. When a financial professional who regularly appears on the media commits to great service for each of his clients, he will raise the bar high and above what they expect. That's the type of service that ideal clients want, and it causes them to refer friends, family, and coworkers to experience the wow factor that you provide.

As you develop yourself as a media expert, always remember that you work for your clients first and for the media second. That is the attitude of a successful financial advisor. You recognize that without your clients, you have no business and no stream of base income. You also realize that without the media, you have no steady stream of new prospective clients coming in your doors. The truly successful advisors I know are committed to providing premium service to their clients. And that service consists not only of actively communicating with them on a frequent basis, but also closely monitoring their investments and helping them gain the investment returns they need to achieve their goals.

Let's think about this from the perspective of clients. The financial advisor (you) meets with them throughout the year, calls them to touch base, regularly e-mails them a financial planning newsletter, and closely monitors their investment performance and recommends changes when necessary. If that weren't enough, their advisor (you) is a recognized financial expert and appears in the media. How much better can it possibly get for your clients?

If you can begin to implement these positive changes in how you run your practice, over time you will become the standard by which the other financial professionals in your local buying area are judged. What a great way to retain the clients you have and to attract the clients of other advisors! As more and more individuals begin investing in the stock market and as those who have been investing see their portfolios grow, they want advisors who will provide them with excellent advice and guidance. If you're committed to staying in business for the long haul and you want to drive up the value of your business for the future, now is the time to begin putting these practices into action.

MEDIA ACTION POINTS

✔ When you appear in the media, celebrate by calling some of your top clients.

✔ Overwhelm your clients with surprisingly great service.

✔ Remember that you work for your clients first and the media second.

BECOMING THE EXPERT

Being the expert means that you're committed not only to appearing regularly in the media, but also to maintaining excellence in your client service. Becoming a financial expert is a lot like beginning a workout program at the gym. At first it's difficult, because you have to change your behavior—you get up early and have to be disciplined enough to get out of bed and go to the gym. (In the same way, getting into the media means adding one more thing to your already busy schedule.) Then you experience soreness from using muscles you haven't used in a while. (Just as it can be difficult to start setting up new systems to provide premium service to your clients.) But after you've been working out for a while, you begin feeling better and looking better. (As you begin implementing your systems to deliver great service, you'll start feeling more confident as a recognized financial advisor and more empowered to go out and acquire new clients.)

CHALLENGE

Put into practice the steps I have laid out for you to capture the attention of reporters and producers. For each interview you do, use the power of mental preparation to enhance your personal execution. Learning how to become a recognized financial expert takes time. Focus your time and energies on every interview as if it were one of your most important goals. And with each of these steps and the more interviews you do, you'll see yourself making progress. Occasionally you will think back to the time when you only dreamed about being in the media. You'd seen other people's interviews or quotes, but you never thought it was possible for you. But that's all changed now. In the same way that an athlete trains and prepares for competition, you must practice and prepare yourself to achieve victory. The more media opportunities you have, the more confident you'll become—and the media will turn to you more and more as the financial expert who can provide timely and relevant financial information for their audience.

CHAPTER FIVE

CREATE
THE BRAND

You're now a regular in the media. People are beginning to recognize you from your appearances, and you're attracting your ideal clients. With each interview, you'll start to develop your own style and feel increasingly comfortable with how you're communicating both to the media and to your audience. As you appear more often, you must understand the importance not only of managing what you say and do, but also of managing the local public's *perception* of you.

Why is this concept so important? Think about the brand names of products you buy and use every day. What did those companies do to make you believe that those products are superior to the competition? Typically, four key factors make you buy one product over another.

1. The product projects an image or "personality" that you like. Through the company's advertising and reputation, you feel good about using that product.

2. The product is of high quality and the leader in its field.

3. It's consistent. It will work or taste the same way today as it did the last time you purchased it.

4. It's accessible. The company has established efficient systems to allow you to purchase the product easily.

Let's review those four factors again: image, quality, consistency, and accessibility. It's interesting that these are also the primary characteristics that clients are looking for in their advisors. Let's take a closer look at each characteristic:

- *Image.* Clients want their advisor to have a professional and likable demeanor. They expect to be able to develop a rapport with their advisor, on both a professional and a personal level.

- *Quality.* They want to work with someone who is knowledgeable and an expert in the field. As clients share their financial secrets, goals, and dreams, they want to feel a high level of trust in their advisor.

- *Consistency.* Clients want to meet in person the same expert they've seen on the media. They also want to feel that the advice they are given is always in their best interest and that their advisor is in touch with their goals.

- *Accessibility.* Clients want their advisor to be reachable. They know that he's frequently on TV, and they may wonder if their call is important enough for him to take. They want their advisor not only to respond to their calls or e-mails quickly, but also to contact them about what is going on in the market and provide ideas to help improve their finances.

These are the key characteristics that give your clients a daily reason to reaffirm that they made a good decision in choosing you.

As I discussed earlier, many financial professionals are known for an attitude of "my way or the highway." They believe that because of what they've done in the past, their clients are now a "captive audience" that will continue to work with them, no matter what. Because many investors have come to expect this type of poor attitude, they stay with these advisors because they feel there are no alternatives.

But times are changing. Financial professionals are beginning to recognize and truly understand how competitive a field financial services is. They realize that their existing clients are bombarded with marketing messages that the grass is greener on another advisor's side of the fence. If you aren't in constant contact with your clients, they may succumb to those messages and meet with another advisor. If that advisor can sell them on what a close relationship they will have and how she will truly listen to their goals and dreams, then the next thing you know, you'll be getting copies of the account transfer paperwork or notice of a canceled life insurance policy. Suddenly you've lost a client and you're left to wonder what happened.

Investors now have a higher level of expectations when they begin working with an advisor. Most accounts that advisors acquire are coming from someone else, such as another advisor who *didn't* adopt a mentality of total service to his or her clients. Clients who are transferring their accounts are jumping ship because they desperately want to work with someone who will care for them and their money. You can be that someone by utilizing your media appearances to deliver the message that you embody the four traits investors are looking for: image, quality, consistency, and accessibility. You need to "brand" yourself as you appear in the media by creating a consistent picture of yourself that includes what people want, and is tailored to the specific group of ideal clients you want to target.

MEDIA ACTION POINTS

✔ Investors are looking for four traits from their advisor: image, quality, consistency, and accessibility.

✔ Clients are leaving advisors who don't embody those traits.

✔ You can create a "brand" in your media appearances that demonstrates that you have those characteristics, and you can tailor that brand to meet the needs of your ideal prospects.

IMAGE

BUILDING A REPUTATION

Think for a moment about someone for whom you have a great deal of respect and admiration. What characteristics best describe that person? Do you find him trustworthy? A good listener? Perhaps he is very wise? Has he repeatedly helped you by giving good advice? Now let's go a little bit deeper. Did the person you're thinking about suddenly become wise this year? Or did you wake up one morning and realize that this person is someone really admirable? Probably not. A positive reputation is something that is built over time.

It takes many years of consistently making the right choices for clients, listening to their needs, and being there for them before financial advisors really can solidify their reputation. Even then, if you're not appearing in the media and don't have a platform for projecting that stellar reputation to a large group of people, it won't matter whether you're the smartest financial advisor in your area. If people can't find you or don't know who you are, you could be out of business before you know it. Part of maintaining your image is to market yourself continually. Always market yourself to your existing clients to get quality introductions to new clients, and always look for ways to utilize the media to target new qualified prospects.

BECOMING THE ADVISOR THEY RELATE TO

The beauty of the media is that it reaches thousands of people, but in a face-to-face way. Think about it. You probably listen to the radio most often when you're in the car by yourself. You generally read the newspaper by yourself. And, in many cases, you may watch the news by yourself while getting ready for work or winding down at your home. For the most part, it's just you and the media. Why is this point important? Because when you're the one appearing in the media, you're essentially having one-on-one time with thousands of people at once. If people are interested in what you have to say, they will really begin to listen to you and process what you're saying. Ideally, if you're doing your job well and people are trusting your advice, they will want to take action.

In order for you to convey an image that prospective clients can relate and respond to, you need to comment on the issues that matter most to them as you appear in the media. The more you do that, the more you will be elevated in their eyes to the status of a financial expert. Table 5.1 shows the three-step process to doing this effectively.

Here's an example of how this process works. Imagine yourself saying this in an interview: "As I visit with new clients each day, they share with me that they are worried about running out of money in retirement. I understand their concerns because I've worked with many people to help them retire successfully. Here are some strategies to consider if you're worried about your retirement. . . ."

In those words, you've identified a major concern of investors (running out of money in retirement). You've expressed that you understand that concern, since you've worked with many people to help them retire. Finally, you've demonstrated that you know how to remove that concern, by presenting them with several concrete strategies to consider. By doing these three things, you've projected the image that you're understanding, experienced, and knowledgeable. You've also captured the attention of people listening or watching you because they share many of those common concerns.

One of the fundamental rules of successful selling is that consumers like to buy from people who are similar to them and who take the time to truly understand their needs. As a consumer, when you begin to get the feeling that salespeople are placing their self-interest above your best interest, it's usually an immediate turnoff. If that happens, the odds of you buying something from those salespeople can plummet. One question new advisors often ask me is

Table 5.1 Empathy Expression Model

Step 1:	Step 2:	Step 3:
Identify their worry.	Express that you understand their worry.	Demonstrate that you know how to remove this worry.

how they can begin to relate to older prospects. They worry that their youthful appearance or minimal experience will be a drawback in securing these people as clients.

How can you overcome either not having a great deal of experience in the financial field or not feeling comfortable in front of older prospects? The best way is to establish credibility through the media. That way when people come into your office to visit with you, they already know what you look like, how you talk, and something of your investment philosophy. From that point on, your job is simply a matter of careful listening, taking notes, and asking a lot of questions to determine their core emotional and financial issues. If you do that successfully, your closing ratio will begin to soar. And in most cases, your youthful appearance will be overlooked because of the credibility you've established.

If a potential client asks your age, you might say, "One of the reasons people decide to have me as their advisor is because of my age. They want a financial professional who understands technology and how the markets and investments work today. They also want to make sure that I'm going to be around for a long time to help them achieve their financial goals." Let's examine what you've said here.

- You have acknowledged that you're young. You're not trying to hide that fact.
- You're stating how your age is actually an asset and not a liability.
- You're subtly communicating the fact that your age and knowledge are primary reasons that they should choose you as their financial professional.

Remember, though, that the credibility you establish through your media appearances will take you only so far. You also must ensure that the image you're projecting is of an advisor who cares about your clients as people. After all, they have come to you because they feel that you might be able to help them. It has been said that "people don't care how much you know until they know how much you care." As you visit with clients, if you come across as interested only in their dollars and not in them as people, you will not experience much success.

To truly maximize your appearances in the media, you must exceed your prospects' expectations. You must present the image that you care more about the people you work with than you do about your media appearances. Let me give you an example. When prospective clients sit down in my office, often they ask about my television appearances: How did I get into television? Do I get a lot of clients from TV? How do I balance being in the media and taking care of my clients? Of course, I answer their questions first. Then I tell them that I enjoy being on television and that I enjoy working with everyone at the station. Most people want me to confirm that the news anchors they watch each day, who seem like nice people on the air, actually are nice people in person. However, despite the fact that I answer prospective clients' questions about how I balance my media appearances with monitoring client portfolios, some still may be concerned that I may be too busy or too successful to take them on as clients.

Although this is a good problem to have, it's critical to address this concern head-on so ideal prospects don't walk out the door without choosing to work with you. What makes this an interesting problem is that few people actually will address it with you. Rather, they hope that during their meeting with you, their concerns will be relieved. But why risk not capitalizing on a great opportunity? I have found that it's best to address this potential concern right up front.

Here's what I say to prospective clients: "John and Mary, because of the work I do in the media, I often get asked about how I can be on TV *and* run a successful business where we take care of all of our clients. You may be thinking the same question. One of the reasons that I do so many interviews is that it forces me to stay sharp. If I have to comment on the latest news on Wall Street or the most recent economic report, it means that I have to be able to explain what it means to the average person. What that means to you, my client, is that I can then take that knowledge and apply it to help benefit your situation. The bottom line is that we try always to stay on top of things so that we can leverage that information for you. Does that make sense? Is that the type of advisor you're looking for?" The most common response I receive is "Yes, that's exactly what we want." Then we begin to go into a deeper discussion about their financial goals and dreams.

By being direct to prospective clients, you've addressed a potential concern and taken away a possible reason for them not to do business with you. You've also positioned all the media work you do as a tremendous advantage that you have over other financial professionals. And you've illustrated the point that your clients are the recipients of the vast knowledge you acquire in preparing for your media interviews. As you meet with prospective clients and they express a financial concern to you, follow these four steps to success.

1. Restate the concern in your own words.

2. Address the concern.

3. Explain the systems or strategies you have put in place so that the concerns are resolved.

4. In meetings with the next prospective client, add these concerns to the issues you bring up when you discuss how you work with people.

Over time, you will cover so many concerns up front that people may have, that they will think you are reading their minds. Doing this will make it even easier for your ideal prospects to decide to work with you.

As people come into your office, remember that you are the specialist, and they are hoping you can diagnose what ails them. They come to your office because they have either seen or heard you in the media or they have been referred to you by someone who trusts you. Either way, you no longer have to tout your own credentials; that's already been done for you. Instead, you can spend your time developing a relationship with these people, helping them identify their fears and concerns and then outlining a plan of how you can help them address those fears and concerns. By the end of the meeting, ask: "How do you feel about what we've discussed?" and "Is this the approach you're looking for?" If they say yes, they have now become clients. You have successfully transitioned those people from prospects (who trusted your image and advice in the media) to clients (who will now trust that image and advice in person).

MEDIA ACTION POINTS

✔ When meeting with prospective clients, identify their worries, state that you understand those worries, and then pose a solution to their worries.

✔ Put at ease people who may be concerned that you are too busy with your media appearances to help them with their financial planning.

Establishing Your Identity

As you are interviewed and appear in the media, reporters and producers will ask what your title is so that you can be properly introduced and identified by the media. Establishing a clear and consistent title is a key part of your image. Let's divide this into two primary categories: print media and television or radio media.

Print Media   When you're quoted in the print media, such as the newspaper or on the Internet, your quote will often look like this:

> "Your comment about the stock market," said (your name), a (your title) with (your company name).

This sounds obvious, but you want to use whatever name you go by, not necessarily your full legal name. When it comes to your title, you have several options to consider. They may include: Chartered Financial Consultant (ChFC), Certified Financial Planner (CFP), Chartered Life Consultant (CLC), Chartered Financial Analyst (CFA), Chartered Retirement Planning Counselor (CRPC), Certified Public Accountant (CPA), and Registered Investment Advisor (RIA). Another set of titles may come from your investment firm, such as Vice President of Investments, Senior Financial Advisor, Investment Representative, or simply Financial Advisor.

I recommend that you use one of your company titles as your first choice, because the public usually recognizes those titles better than professional designations from the financial services industry. Thus, you would use this format:

> "Your quote about the stock market," said Susan Jones, an investment representative with ABC Financial.

The reading public already has a clear picture of what an "investment representative" is, so that's the better title to go with, even if Susan Jones is also a CFP.

Whichever title you choose, it's important to use that title consistently. Remember that your goal is to become recognized as a financial expert in your local area. To do that, you must keep things simple: both your message and your title. Choose a title that you feel best fits how you want to be known, and then stick with it.

Television/Radio Media   Being introduced by the television and radio media is a different story. Because what you say is not in print, your contacts in this media typically are looking for an angle for their guests that is catchy, so it will grab their audience's attention. They are also more likely to introduce you as a financial expert, because they want their audience to feel that their station has the experts on any given topic. When producers ask for your title, consider telling them to introduce you as: "(Your name), a financial expert with (your company name)."

People want to work with a financial expert, and most people clearly understand that when the word "expert" is used, it means that you are an authority on your subject. We all want to work with the best. The use of the word "expert" gives the impression that you are an intelligent and highly credible source for financial information.

MEDIA ACTION POINTS

✔ For print media, choose a title that is simple and that the average reader can understand easily.

✔ For television and radio, consider using the title "financial expert."

✔ For all your media appearances, be consistent with your title.

FINDING YOUR NICHE

In addition to nailing down a title, another important aspect of establishing a clear image is to identify your specific target market and describe whom you work with in one sentence. This sentence is known as a niche positioning statement. For example, here's what I tell people when they ask me about the types of clients I have: "I specialize in working with clients who are a few years from retirement or already retired." That comment typically opens the door for people to ask more questions about how I work with people, what kind of advice I give them, and so on.

Weaving this niche positioning statement into your media interviews can be very powerful, especially when you're appearing on TV or on the radio and your comments are not being edited as in a newspaper article. You can say something such as: "As I work with clients who are a few years from retirement or already retired, one of the biggest concerns they have is how they can use their investments to generate a monthly paycheck." By utilizing your niche positioning statement in your media appearances, you can solidify your image as an advisor who works with a specific group of clients. Your target market of prospects will pay closer attention to what you're saying when they find out you specialize in working with people like them.

Now it's time for you to create some niche positioning statements for yourself. Here are some examples:

- *Debt focus.* "I specialize in working with clients who are aggressively working to pay off their debt so they can begin investing for the future."

- *Education focus.* "I specialize in working with clients who want to provide their children with the best college education possible while remaining within their budget."

- *Pre-retirement focus.* "I specialize in helping clients create the retirement lifestyle they've always dreamed about."

- *Retired focus.* "I specialize in helping retired clients do what they want to do, when they want to do it, without the fear of running out of money."

- *Tax focus.* "I specialize in helping clients take full advantage of the current tax laws, so that Uncle Sam is working for them and not against them."

Creating a niche positioning statement is simple. Just write down the words "I specialize" and then, in one short sentence, write down the focus of your business. Use this template to create your own niche positioning statement:

> I specialize in helping clients (*or* working with clients) (insert the primary benefit you provide to people here.)

The more you begin saying this positioning statement to people, the more it will keep you focused on the ideal prospects you're seeking, and the more it will attract them to work with you.

In building your brand, it's all about consistency and staying focused. Over time, you want to become known as the expert in your field. As you develop your niche positioning statement, make sure it's something that sounds authentic and that you're comfortable saying it. If it sounds too slick or salesy, it will have the opposite effect from what you've intended and will turn away potential clients instead of attracting them.

MEDIA ACTION POINTS

✔ Create a niche positioning statement that will appeal to your ideal prospects.

✔ Find ways to weave your positioning statement into your media appearances.

QUALITY

How to Set Yourself Apart

When it comes to working with a financial professional, investors have countless choices. There are financial planners, financial advisors, insurance professionals, accountants, and stockbrokers. How can you stand out as the person people call on? You can do so by positioning yourself as a recognized expert who can offer quality advice in a few specific areas.

Why will such specification help you stand out to potential clients? Think about your health as an example. If you had a serious medical condition, would you be comfortable going to a general practitioner, who had a little bit of knowledge about everything, or would you prefer to go straight to a specialist, whose focus and expertise was in your specific problem? Of course, we would all choose to meet with the specialist, because we feel that person would have more recent and relevant experience in helping others with the same medical problem. The same line of reasoning holds true when investors are selecting a financial professional. They can choose either a generalist financial advisor or a specialist financial advisor.

Generalist financial advisors present themselves to the public as knowing a little bit about everything. Financial issues that generalists might cover include:

- Helping clients save for their first home
- Showing clients how to get out of debt
- Setting up accounts for clients to save for their child's education
- Helping clients begin to save for retirement

The problem that generalist financial advisors face is that they typically attract less savvy investors, who have less money to invest and are less likely to buy other investment products, such as insurance and annuities. As a result, generalists often have less profitable practices than specialists.

Specialist financial advisors can attract and focus on investors who meet their specific criteria. Clients of specialists often are interested in having a custom-tailored plan to help them reach their specific financial goals. Specialists who focus on clients who are close to retirement and have portfolios worth $250,000 or more, for example, might cover these issues for clients:

- Transitioning a person's growth portfolio to a retirement income portfolio

- Helping clients prepare financially, emotionally, and psychologically for moving from earning a paycheck to beginning their retirement
- Creating a plan for clients to achieve the steady level of income they want in retirement
- Working with a client's estate planning attorney and tax accountant to explore charitable gifting strategies

Transitioning your practice to that of a specialist will allow you to develop a niche—an area of specific and exclusive focus. The other benefit of becoming a specialist is that it allows you to work with only those clients who have similar considerations. By doing so, your professional development will deepen quickly and your knowledge base will increase, because you're focusing solely on a few specific client needs. With each client you work with, you become more and more of an expert in your area of focus. Plus, as your reputation begins to grow, other financial professionals may begin referring people to you, as you are now the expert in a specific area.

MEDIA ACTION POINTS

✔ Decide to be a specialist financial advisor, not a generalist.

✔ Choose a specific area of expertise that suits you and that will be profitable for your practice.

When you appear in the media, you want to project yourself as a specialist who can provide high-quality advice in your area of expertise. You want to stand out from the countless financial professionals who compete for your target prospects' business. How can you stand out? By discussing topics that are of concern to people in your target market. Choose topics and pick phrases that will resonate with those people. If you choose to target people who are close to retirement, here are some "power phrases" to include when you appear in the media:

- "As I visit with prospective clients in my office about their retirement concerns, some of the things they share with me are . . ."
- "As I meet with people, I have found that the closer they get to retirement, the more worried they are about having enough money. Here's what I tell them to think about . . ."
- "If you're retired, there are some things you should consider to ensure that you don't run out of money in retirement. They are . . ."
- "I'm often asked how people should invest their money once they retire. Here are some things to consider . . ."
- "Many people are worried about how they're going to put their children through school and still enjoy the retirement they want. Here are some strategies for you to consider . . ."

Tweak these models to fit whatever area you decide to specialize in. Once you determine the area in which you want to be perceived as the specialist, simply practice giving responses like the ones just given and insert your particular topic of expertise into them. For example: "I find that many people are worried about (fill in topic). Here are some things to consider if you are worried about (fill in topic)."

Here are some additional phrases you can say to capture a prospective client's attention:

- "Let's say that you've just moved into the (insert city name) area. Here is what new residents often ask me . . ."
- "If you have money in the stock market, here's something that you need to be aware of . . ."
- "If you're worried about how to pay for your child's education, listen to this . . ."
- "If you've been offered an early retirement package, here's what you need to consider . . ."
- "If you need more income from your investments, here are some things to think about . . ."

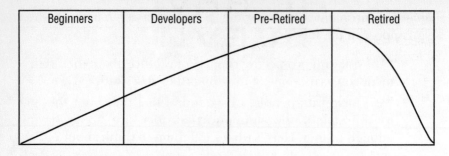

| Beginners | Developers | Pre-Retired | Retired |

Figure 5.1   Four Investor Types

The audience you decide to target will determine what key messages you convey. For the sake of this discussion, I've divided investors into four primary categories: Beginners, Developers, Preretired, and Retired. Figure 5.1 demonstrates how assets generally are accumulated within these groups.

If you decided to specialize in the needs of Beginners, you'd want to keep the following points in Table 5.2 in mind.

Developers face their own unique challenges and will respond to different topics as shown in Table 5.3.

If you'd like to work with the Preretired market, consider Table 5.4.

The final group of investors is the Retired market, shown in Table 5.5.

Table 5.2   Investment Concerns of Beginner Investors

Common Issues for Beginners	"Hot Buttons" to Discuss for Beginners
• Budgeting for initial purchases • Buying a car • Beginning a new job • Getting married • Buying a first home • Having a child	• Getting a great deal on a car • What to consider when changing companies or starting a new job • Working together financially when you get married • What to consider before buying a home • Preparing your monthly budget for a new child

Table 5.3   Investment Concerns of Developer Investors

Common Issues for Developers	"Hot Buttons" to Discuss for Developers
• Paying off debt • Saving for children's education • Economic impact of having more children • Upgrading to a larger home • Searching for direction in their career field	• Strategies for getting out of debt with a growing family • The best ways to save for college • What to do before you move into a bigger house • What you need to know before jumping ship to a new company

Table 5.4   Investment Concerns of Pre-Retired Investors

Common Issues for the Preretired Market	"Hot Buttons" to Discuss for the Preretired Market
• Preparing for retirement • Children in college • Balancing paying for college and saving for retirement • Parents getting older and needing assistance for retirement • Paying off debt	• Retirement strategies to save more money if you're behind the curve • How much does it really cost to send your child to college? • How much should you be saving for retirement? • Strategies to prepare your investments

Table 5.5   Investment Concerns of Retired Investors

Common Issues for the Retired Market	"Hot Buttons" to Discuss for the Retired Market
• Outliving their money • Having enough money to do what they want • Increases in medical and prescription drug costs • The possibility of a stay in a nursing home • Dependent children	• How to prevent your money from running out • Portfolio strategies to help generate steady income with minimal risks • What to consider when working part-time in retirement • Long-term care insurance • Getting your estate in order

MEDIA ACTION POINTS

✔ During your interviews, use "power phrases" that will appeal to your target market.

✔ Speak about topics that will interest your target market.

✔ Become an expert in all the topics that interest your target market.

THE TRUST FACTOR

As you appear in the media more frequently, you will begin to develop a reputation. The quality of that reputation will depend on how you come across in the various media outlets. That reputation will be the primary factor that potential clients consider as they decide whether to give you a call and meet with you.

How do people that I've never met before begin perceiving me as trustworthy? What am I saying or doing that causes people to feel that they would be comfortable investing their hard-earned dollars with me? Here's the answer I've come up with: Over time, as I have appeared in the media each week, I have tried to be consistent, to speak clearly, and to inject humor when appropriate. I've also kept in mind that during my media appearances, I am the expert and I am the one that thousands of people are counting on to deliver relevant financial information. I take this responsibility very seriously, and that fact comes across both to the media contacts that I work with and, more important, to their audiences.

The great news is that you have the same opportunity to establish a reputation as a high-quality advisor. As you appear in the media more, you will begin to develop your own style and communication methods. But always remember that it all comes down to the trust factor. As people begin to trust you as a credible source for timely and relevant financial information, you can become the recognized financial expert in your local area. When people are ready to work with a quality financial professional, you can be the one they call. The beauty of establishing yourself as a trustworthy person is that when prospective clients come into your office, they will have no suspicion or doubt about you. They'll figure that if you're in the media, you know what you're doing (and you shouldn't attempt to be in the media if you *don't* know what you're doing), and they'll assume that you're a good source for sound financial planning.

As you begin to get more comfortable being interviewed and appearing in the media, it's important to remember that the first step to being recognized as a trustworthy and authentic advisor to your audience is simply to be yourself. Think about your current clients. Why do they work with you? It's most likely because you're knowledgeable, personable, have a sense of humor, and are easy to work with. Those are the same characteristics that will help you be successful in your media endeavors. The mistake I see many financial professionals making is that they think they have to come across as someone different when they appear in the media. There are two dangers in doing this. By trying to appear smarter than you are or by using complex financial words when you speak, you actually can seem to be talking down to your audience. Also, you don't want to seem one way in the media and then seem completely different when prospective clients meet you in person. One of the greatest ways to leverage the media is to presell you to your prospective clients. When they come into your office, what they see should be what they get.

MEDIA ACTION POINTS

✔ Be the same person in the media as you are when you meet with people.

✔ Think about the qualities that caused your current clients to work with you, then leverage those attributes in the media.

✔ Explain financial topics in an easy-to-understand way.

RESIST THE URGE TO SELL ON THE AIR

When you talk with the media, be careful never, directly or indirectly, to sell your company's products as you are being interviewed.

Any attempt to sell your products will be a major turnoff to your media contacts, because it will appear that you are directly working the media for your own financial gain. It also sends the message to the audience that you may not be an impartial source for timely financial information, but rather a product salesperson disguised as a financial professional. As tempted as you may be to mention the specific names of financial products you have available, don't do it. Instead, speak in more general terms. For example, don't say, "(Your company name) mutual fund is a great recommendation." Instead, speak in broader terms: "Mutual funds can be a good option for many investors. A person's age and risk tolerance will determine whether it's best to invest in growth funds. Typically, a well-diversified portfolio works best." You can speak on clearly factual information, such as a just-released company's earnings report or an economic report. However, be careful not to give your personal opinion on a company or its stock; doing that may be perceived as recommending it.

From a compliance standpoint, it's always best to speak in general terms. It's also important to remember not to solicit viewers or listeners to call you to schedule a meeting. As you're appearing as the expert, you'll be tempted to ask people to come in right away and meet with you. However, resist that temptation. Don't say, "If you have questions about this, please call me at my office and I'll be happy to meet with you." That can come across as self-serving, and it implies that you work with everyone who calls. Instead, get into the habit of saying one of these options:

- "This investment option may or may not be appropriate for your specific situation. It's best to consult with a qualified financial advisor who specializes in these types of investments."

- "Everyone's situation is different. If you're working with a financial advisor now, call him or her and ask whether this strategy is appropriate for you."

- "While this strategy may sound great, it's best to consult with a financial, tax, or legal professional before implementing these ideas."

Why are these statements better than directly telling people to call you? There are three reasons.

1. You've appeared objective to the media outlet and to its audience. It doesn't want someone self-promoting.

2. You've suggested that people work closely with their current financial professionals.

3. You have conveyed the message that you are a specialist and you are selective about whom you decide to take on as a client. By subtly "playing hard to get" and not coming across as if you're begging people to work with you, you can make your ideal prospects want to work with you even more. This strategy works for me and it can work for you, too! The only exception to this rule is if you have your own radio program as discussed in Chapter Three. Because you are paying for that time, you can be more direct in how you approach prospective clients.

MEDIA ACTION POINTS

✔ Don't mention your company's specific products in your interviews.

✔ Resist the urge to solicit business when you're on the air.

✔ By suggesting people consult with a qualified financial professional, they will often choose to work with you.

CONSISTENCY

CONVEYING A CONSISTENT MESSAGE

As I discussed earlier, as you begin appearing in the media, it is crucial that you convey a consistent message in every interview. Keep in mind that your goal in appearing in the media is to allow your audience to develop an invisible rapport with you over time. Some people may see you on television while they are on the treadmill at the gym. Others may see your name in the newspaper with their morning coffee. Still others may hear you on the radio as they drive to and from work. The key is that over time, they begin to accept you as a credible source for timely financial information.

Think back to Chapter One when I discussed the Marketing Continuum and the three phases of how people gradually accept you as "their" financial advisor before they've even met you. As your media appearances continue, a gradual evolution will take place in the minds of your audience. Eventually they begin to recognize you and then trust you as a source of key economic information and valuable stock market perspective. That evolution is complete when they become your clients. But the evolution is disrupted if you are inconsistent—if you are different in person from how you are in the media, or if you present an inconsistent image in your media appearances.

Psychologists tell us that it's human nature to want consistency in our lives. In our relationships with our family, friends, and coworkers, we want to be able to count on people to be relatively the same, day in and day out. We carry that same desire over to other aspects of our lives as well. As we absorb information on a daily basis, we continue to seek out consistency, directly and indirectly. For example, if you ask people about their favorite TV programs, they're likely not only to rattle off a list of shows, but also to describe some of their favorite episodes or even to quote one-liners. Why is that? It's because when we find something we like, we often accept it wholeheartedly and make it part of our lives and culture. The same holds true when you ask people which local news channel they like to watch. For most, their feelings about specific people in the media—whether it's a television anchor, a radio show host, or a newspaper reporter—determine whether they decide to watch, listen, or read that particular channel or publication.

When I open up the Sunday newspaper, for example, there are certain sections I go to first and certain columnists I read first. Why do I do that? It's because I like their style and viewpoint, and the way they write makes sense to me. Over the years, I've come to rely on these particular writers for timely and interesting articles. Every week I can count on them to write an article that is thought-provoking and appealing to me. The same holds true for you when you're doing interviews. As you appear in the media, consistency in what you say and do is critical to your long-term success. As you begin to appear regularly, you will begin to develop a following. Some people will begin to look forward to reading your quotes in the newspaper, watching you on TV, or listening to you on the radio. By consistently commenting on timely financial news in your unique style, you will be establishing a firm foundation of marketing that you can build on for many years to come and regularly attract new ideal clients.

STAYING IN FRONT OF THEM

With so much going on in our lives, it's common for us to forget what is not always right in front of us. It's easy for your clients to lose focus of things that were once very important to them. Think about when you first meet with prospective clients. They are highly motivated to take action to achieve their financial goals. During the initial stages of your relationship, you're talking to them frequently and your time with them is very interactive. Then you create a financial plan to help them reach their objectives. They're excited to see in black and white what it will take to reach their financial goals. They implement the plan you have created, investing money with you or purchasing insurance policies to help solve their problems. They're very motivated. They've taken action and they feel good about it. However, over time, clients can get distracted due to life events. Some get married, remarried, divorced, lose a job, find a new job, or move to another part of the country. Because of everything that occurs in their lives, it's easy for them to begin to lose sight of the importance of continuing to save for their financial goals.

If you want your clients to stay motivated and to continue working toward their financial goals, you as their advisor must stay in touch with them and in front of them continually. Investor research consistently shows that the financial professionals who are in regular contact with their clients experience the most success, not only in keeping their clients but also in having clients invest more money with them. Keep in mind that the same life events that cause clients to lose sight of their goals are occurring in the lives of your prospective clients as well. If you want to make even minimal gains in capturing their attention, you must develop a plan to appear in the media on a regular basis. You want to be a name or a face or a voice that people become used to seeing, so that they will begin to accept you. That consistency will propel you to the status of a trusted financial expert, and it's what will make your name the first one people think of when they decide to get help with their investments.

Simply put, prospective clients are a lot like popcorn. When you put a bag of popcorn kernels in the microwave, what happens? As the bag begins to heat up, suddenly one kernel pops and then another and then another, until the entire bag is full of popped corn for you to enjoy. The more you appear in the media, and the more you "turn up the heat" on your prospective clients, the more uncomfortable they will become with their own financial situation. Just like the kernels that pop randomly, prospective clients who want to meet with you will begin popping up all over your area because what you're saying makes sense to them. Whether you're being interviewed in the television studio or meeting with a reporter, remember that good things happen when you're in front of people.

MEDIA ACTION POINTS

✔ Be consistent in your message and your image as you appear in the media.

✔ Seek out repeat appearances.

✔ Being in front of people in person and through the media causes good things to happen for your business.

THE LOCAL CELEBRITY

You know you're doing a good job consistently promoting yourself through the media when people begin to tell you that they have seen you or your name somewhere. It is especially gratifying when business and civic leaders whom you respect comment that they enjoy seeing you on the news or in the newspaper. When this first happens, it may catch you off guard and you may not know how to respond. I have discovered the best response is to simply say "Thank you very much. I appreciate that," or "Thank you. I enjoy getting to do that." This response conveys a humble attitude and a sense that you're in the media all the time but it's not a big deal to you. The more low key you are about it, the more attractive you become as an advisor people want to work with, and the more you stand out to them as a true financial professional. This is the power of the media selling you to people so you don't have to sell yourself.

Many of us have the perception that those in the media are "larger than life." As you appear in the media more frequently, people will begin to have that same perception about you. The way to leverage that perception is by remaining personable and down-to-earth despite your success. After all, just because you're appearing regularly in the media, the money isn't necessarily flying in your door yet. It takes time to start seeing the payoff in your pocketbook. If you are perceived as the financial expert, and if when people meet with you they are impressed by how friendly and caring you are, very likely they will choose to work with you. The media has presold them on your knowledge and trustworthiness. Now all you have to do is be consistent and let your prospective clients connect the "recognized financial expert" with the warm, caring, and articulate financial advisor they meet in person—that's when your media exposure begins to help generate dollars for you and your business.

The beauty of media outlets is that they do the work for you in creating the highest level of visibility and credibility possible, so you don't have to toot your own horn. Behind the scenes, you are working diligently to stay in the public eye and developing new ways to keep your name and face in front of people through the media. Each week you're sending your faxes and e-mails to the media to capture their attention so they'll pick you for interviews. You're aggressively pursuing every possible opportunity to get in front of the media's audience. Publicly you are providing excellent client service and financial planning advice to your clients and are attracting a steady stream of prospective clients. The general public and your current clients have no idea that you're actually working as your own public relations firm behind the scenes to create all of your media opportunities. They just think the media magically called you one day out of the blue because you're a top-notch financial professional. It's okay to let them think that. But you know all the hard work you have done, and now you're reaping what you have sown. To your clients and prospective clients, you have positioned yourself as being irresistible to work with. You're like a magnet that easily attracts ideal clients. Let's look at this more closely. You appear in the media all the time. You come across as knowledgeable and down-to-earth. And to top if off, you're a nice, caring professional in person. Those are the ingredients that spell success.

The other benefit that often occurs is that when you are in a group of people, someone may say that they saw you in the newspaper or on television and everyone's ears will perk up. They realize that they are in the presence of a local celebrity. People will ask what you do and about the types of clients you have. And the best thing of all is that you weren't the one bragging about yourself and your accomplishments—the media did it for you! Your media work provides a great opportunity for people who haven't met you yet to say to themselves, "Wow, this person really knows what she is doing!" Remember that you can't develop this type of reputation overnight. It's built over time, week in and week out, as you work to become known as a knowledgeable and approachable person who consistently gives great financial advice.

MEDIA ACTION POINTS

✔ Be the same expert in person that your prospects have seen in the media.

✔ Show humility as people begin to recognize you as a local celebrity.

✔ Let the media toot your horn about what a great financial professional you are.

BECOMING A HOUSEHOLD NAME

The frequency of your media appearances will determine how much name recognition you develop. For every famous person you know who seems to have had a lucky break, I can guarantee you there is a behind-the-scenes story of a long climb to success. Your situation will be similar. After all, it may take months to land your first media appearance and perhaps even years before you land a regular, consistent appearance on a specific television or radio program. The same holds true as you begin to be interviewed by your local newspaper or you begin submitting a byline financial column for it to print on a regular basis. It's all about consistency and frequency. As prospective clients see your name in print, read your perspective on financial issues, see your face or hear your voice, and hear you conveying the same message over and over, they will be more likely to take notice when you appear.

Think back to the first chapter when we discussed the concept of capturing the mind share of a client. The more times people see your name somewhere, the more you are becoming recognized, directly and indirectly, as a financial expert. How can you get to that level? By consistently following the plan I have laid out for you. Faithfully implement the media follow-up system each week until you see results. Once you do your first interview, continue to execute the system. As you begin to experience success, don't get lazy or rest on your laurels. From this point on, taking your marketing efforts to a whole new level will require you simply continue to apply the system in your local area. And like countless advisors I have consulted with all over the country, you too will become one of the experts the media calls on.

How to Insulate Your Media Career

Many advisors I talk to fail to understand that just because they have appeared in the media once, that doesn't mean that they've "made it" and they've got a lock on that particular media outlet. Let me shoot straight with you. That line of reasoning can reason you right out of the media. Remember that things are always changing in the media. For example, the primary reporter with whom you have been working may be offered an opportunity to write for a different part of the paper or take a newspaper job elsewhere in the country. Suddenly the person you've built a relationship with is gone, replaced by someone from a competing newspaper with his own list of financial professionals to contact.

It's up to you to introduce yourself to him and convince him to add you to his list of experts. To be successful in your local media over the long term, you have to get used to reintroducing yourself to new reporters and producers and proving yourself over and over again. Over time you will begin to develop a reputation as being a team player who is always willing to do what the media asks. When you've created a name like that for yourself, you're on the pathway to big-time media exposure.

There are two important aspects of becoming a recognized name. First, you want prospective clients to remember your name as a trusted financial expert. You also want the media outlets in your area to think of you as an indispensable part of what they provide to their audience. And second, as a financial expert who is both knowledgeable and an excellent communicator. As you begin to appear more and more on a particular station, for example, aim to have other media outlets vying for your services. If there is ever a management shake-up at the station where you appear, you'll be comforted to know that you can switch to a different station because of the reputation you've established.

The key point to remember is that in the media, nothing is forever. You must constantly be promoting yourself and highly visible to different people at your local media outlets. In the same way that great products become recognized and trusted brand names over time, you can develop a consistent reputation as someone who is a team player and who works well with the media.

ACCESSIBILITY

RELATING TO DIFFERENT PEOPLE

Early on in this business, I realized that to attract a steady stream of ideal clients, I needed to learn how to relate effectively to a wide cross-section of people. I also quickly understood that each ideal client I began working with had a different personality and social style. Each individual has different goals, dreams, and concerns. Although all prospective clients have money to invest, insurance needs to cover, or tax issues to handle, if you want to attract quality clients, you must position yourself as a specialist who can provide them with individual attention. Because each person is different, each person's financial plan should be different too. It's very effective to tell prospects that if they are looking to work with a financial professional who provides a cookie-cutter approach, you are not the person for them. Convey the message that you specialize in providing custom-tailored financial planning services to your clients.

There are many ways to demonstrate that you care about your clients as individuals. For example, the next time you're in front of prospects or current clients and you've presented an idea they need to make a decision about, don't ask them what they "think" about it. Instead, ask them how they "feel" about it. Asking people to think about something can lead to an analytical evaluation, which can lead to procrastination and the avoidance of a clear decision. However, by asking them how they feel about an issue, you can get your clients to focus on the personal aspect of the decision. It comes across as less threatening and gets them to open up more about what they really feel are the drawbacks and benefits to what you're recommending. Asking people how they feel about something also helps set you apart from other "salespeople." I'll detail this more in the next chapter.

MEDIA ACTION POINTS

- ✔ Position yourself as providing custom-tailored financial planning solutions, not a cookie-cutter approach.

- ✔ Learn to relate to a wide cross-section of prospective clients.

- ✔ Be interested in your prospects. Ask the right questions and ask how they "feel" instead of what they "think."

THE NEXT STEPS

Do the Research

Once you've created a "brand" for yourself that embodies the four characteristics—image, quality, consistency, and accessibility—that

your ideal clients are looking for, it's time to determine how well
you've established your brand. As I've discussed throughout this
book, appearing in the media and enjoying the success it brings
takes time and a focused effort. The more often you are seen or
heard by people, the more aware of who you are they become. After you've been appearing in the media for about six months, it's
very important to evaluate what you're doing and what results
you're achieving. One of the best ways to do this is to conduct a
third-party survey. I have hired a professional marketing company
to contact random people in my target market and ask them questions, including:

- Do you currently work with a financial advisor?
- Name some financial planning companies.
- Name some financial advisors.
- What are you most worried about financially right now?
- What are your feelings about (insert your name)?

The purpose of this survey is for you to spot-check what people
in your local area are thinking and feeling. This information will
tell you where you rank in terms of name recognition and also gives
you a barometer on the current "hot buttons" that people have
about their money. Then you can use this information to come up
with seminar presentations or topics for future presentations. See
Table 5.6.

When I work with professionals, I expect them to display a
high attention to detail and a genuine interest in me. Hearing
other people commenting favorably about a product or service I

Table 5.6   Relating Effectively to the Media Audience

If you appear in the media and speak about topics that aren't relevant to people . . . ———▶	you'll be noticed but not paid attention to.
If you appear in the media and speak about feelings and concerns that people have about their money . . . ———▶	you'll be noticed *and* paid attention to.

use or a professional I have consulted with serves to reinforce that I made a good decision. This same thought process holds true when people are selecting a financial professional. They're careful and deliberate in their decision-making process. They continue that process even after they've selected their financial professional. As your clients are talking with their friends or colleagues at work about money issues, they are comparing inwardly the service and advice you provide to that of their friends' financial advisors. They're always seeking validation that they made the right choice.

Here's where your marketing research can pay off in a big way. After you've been appearing in the media for a while and people are commenting regularly that they see your appearances, conduct a survey using the questions I've listed. When you get your marketing analysis back, examine how highly you were ranked in the survey. If you were identified as one of the most recognized financial professionals in your local area, then send a press release to the local media outlets. Position your ranking in your marketing materials to elevate your standing even further with the media and, most important, with your current clients and prospective clients.

- If your name is at the top of the list in name recognition, say: "In a recent survey of investors, (insert your name) was named *the* 'most recognized financial professional' in the (insert city name) area."
- If your name is one of the top names mentioned in the name recognition survey, say: "In a recent survey of investors, (insert your name) was named *one of the* 'most recognized financial professionals' in the (insert city name) area."
- If your name is not identified at all in the survey, assess your media efforts and evaluate what else you could be doing to generate more positive and memorable name recognition for you and your business.

Being the top name mentioned or one of the most recognized names on the survey can provide a huge boost in how you promote yourself. You can leverage your marketing research in these ways:

- Let the anchors who interview you on television or the radio know so they can mention this on the air.
- Add the results as a headline on your web site.
- Add the results to the marketing brochure that you mail to prospective clients.
- Send a press release to the newspaper with the survey results.
- Include the results as part of your introduction at your seminars and public speeches.

MEDIA ACTION POINTS

✔ Hire a marketing company to do a survey on your name recognition.

✔ Learn whether your media work is creating name recognition for you.

✔ Leverage your marketing research findings to generate even more media coverage.

SOLIDIFYING YOUR PERSONAL BRAND

It's important to do more than just appear in the media. You want to take the next step. For example, let's say that you have just been quoted in today's newspaper. You can leverage that one media appearance to multiply it over and over to your clients and prospects.

Here are some ways to maximize your newspaper interviews:

- E-mail the newspaper article's link to your clients with a note that says, "I want to keep you updated on timely financial topics. Here is an article I thought you might find of interest. Thanks, (your name)."

- E-mail the newspaper article's link to your prospect database with a note that says, "Here is an article that I thought you might find of interest. If you have questions about your financial situation, please call our office to schedule a visit. Thanks, (your name)."

- Mail a copy of the newspaper article to your top prospects and clients with your name and quote highlighted with a marker and a note that reads, "Thinking of you. Thought you would find this of interest.—(your name)."

- Keep a leather-bound notebook in your reception area that contains your quotes or press clippings for people to look at when they come to your office.

- Continue to add the different media outlets you have appeared in to your bio letter to establish your credibility.

- On all your marketing materials, include the tagline, "As seen on/in (media outlet name)."

The purpose of these strategies is to build your personal credibility and exposure. You're letting the media brag for you and establish your brand as a financial expert. These are all subtle ways to convey to your clients that they are working with the right person. They also give prospective clients more reasons to begin working with you. Remember, your primary purpose in securing media exposure is to capitalize on the power of the media's third-party endorsement. Once you've established yourself in the media channels you've been working in, it's time to expand to other channels. Now that you have the credibility, start looking into other opportunities that also target your ideal prospects. Perhaps you could appear on other programs, be interviewed by other newspapers or publications, or be a part of other special events. Use the newfound media relationships that you have cultivated to springboard to new opportunities.

As you begin to appear in the media more frequently, it is critical for you to be aware of the ratings of the media outlets you're working with. Make it your goal, over time, to appear in those outlets with the highest level of readers and viewers. As I discussed earlier, when you first begin, *any* media exposure that you get is positive because it allows you to gain experience and get your name out there. But eventually, to build yourself up into a truly recognized local brand, you will need to be associated with the most highly rated media outlets in your local area.

When I first placed byline financial columns in my local newspapers, I began with the local suburban newspaper and then moved to the business newspaper. When I began doing television, I started off on the number-three rated TV station, then went to number-two, and now I am on the number-one rated morning news program. I had contacted all the stations, but it was the luck of the draw that the CBS affiliate contacted me first. I've taken it step-by-step all the way to the media outlets I appear in now. The key is to not be paralyzed by fear of the huge "media monster." Begin to attack it bit by bit and soon you'll experience progress, which will cause your confidence and positive exposure to build.

MEDIA ACTION POINTS

✔ Make the most of your media appearances by sending e-mails and clippings to clients and prospects.

✔ Expand your current appearances by looking for new opportunities.

✔ Work to appear on the highest-rated programs.

COMMUNITY INVOLVEMENT

One of the best ways to solidify your brand is to be highly visible and involved in your local buying community. Whether it is your local Rotary Club or church organization or other business or charitable cause, get involved. Once people begin seeing the "recognized financial expert" as a real person who takes time out of his very busy schedule to help give back to the community, you'll be elevated in their eyes as a respected and admired businessperson. Pick something that you enjoy doing and get as involved as you can without sacrificing your primary objective of growing your business. Your involvement will allow you to take a step back and focus some of your energies on building relationships with others who are focused on a common goal of improving your community.

If people sense your sincerity in being part of the organization through this community involvement, they are likely to ask how you work with clients and may decide to meet with you to help them manage their financial issues. Your goal is to build a reputation as a successful businessperson whom the media has designated as their financial expert and as a person of integrity willing to give back to the community. When you achieve that type of reputation, it becomes very easy for affluent clients to be attracted to you. However, a strong word of caution here: Don't join an organization or get involved in a cause with the primary goal of getting business and lining your own pockets. People will see right through you, and you may do more harm than good to your reputation.

One of the many benefits of joining an organization like the Rotary Club or Kiwanis is the opportunity to meet and visit with other business and community leaders. By asking questions, you can glean information from these leaders and learn from their experiences in the "school of hard knocks." The more you get to know these people, the more opportunities you will have to work with them on special projects, and that can lead to an increased friendship and a level of trust that will enhance greatly your chances of acquiring them as clients.

Remember that your goal is to leverage your status as a local celebrity. The more you appear in the media, the more the influential people in your community will begin to know your name and face. The more visible you are in the community, the more opportunities you give people to connect the media personality with your true personality and to realize what a friendly, knowledgeable, and personable individual you are in real life. And that is when your sales will begin to increase. As I discussed earlier, everyone wants to work with an expert. After all, investments represent countless years of savings and sacrifice. Ideal clients don't want to hand over the reins of their portfolios to just anyone. They want to work with someone whom they feel truly understands them, can empathize with their financial concerns, and will help them achieve their financial dreams for themselves and their families.

MEDIA ACTION POINTS

✔ Pick an organization or cause that you believe in and get involved in your community.

✔ Take advantage of opportunities for people to see that even as a local celebrity, you are personable and easy to work with on special projects.

REVEAL YOUR PERSONAL SIDE

As you develop your status as a financial expert through the media, don't underestimate the importance of showing that you are well rounded. Not only are you up-to-date on the latest financial planning ideas and tools, but you also have a life and interests outside of the office. Time and time again, when clients come into my office and see all the pictures of my family, they immediately realize that my wife and children are very important to me. It's also smart to have a few loose pictures lying around to show to your clients. Here's what I do. When I am talking about my kids to prospective clients, I hand them a few pictures. Having them hold and look at pictures of my kids is a powerful way for them to develop a bond with me and to establish a solid working relationship. Family pictures are also great conversation pieces. In my experience, people like to see the family pictures of the professionals with whom they work. When clients visually see those pictures, it connects to their emotional side and elevates you from a "salesperson" to a respected professional who has both a nice family and a nice business.

Here are some ways to show your personal side in your office:

- Prominently display pictures of your spouse and children and a nice family picture.
- Display awards that you've received.
- Keep a few unframed pictures of your kids that you can hand to clients to see up close.

HAVE THE OFFICE THEY EXPECT

One of your responsibilities as a financial expert is to have an office that meets or exceeds the expectations of the clients or prospective clients who come in your door. Think about the last time you visited the office of your attorney or accountant. Your first impression was probably that it was a very professional office. It was what you would expect from a professional. However, many financial professionals have missed the boat on this one. Their offices have stacks of paper everywhere, client files strewn around, and generally look disorganized. How would you feel if you walked into an office like that? The first impression that people have of your office is powerful and helps set the stage of whether they will work with you.

Let's divide this discussion into two areas: the lobby (the "decompression center" and "stress-release zone") and your office (an "oasis" with no financial gobbledygook). When people walk into your office lobby, you want them to relax. You want to create an environment where people can be removed from the pressures of their daily lives. You want them sitting in a comfortable chair, drinking a beverage, reading a nice travel magazine, and relaxing. That way, when they enter your personal office, they are mentally prepared to do business with you. You spend the time they are in your office working to deepen the relationship. I have found that advisors who have nicer, more upscale offices attract nicer, more affluent clients. Most affluent clients enjoy nice things and want to work with someone who has created an office where they feel special and relaxed.

A financial planner's lobby should not contain:

- Financial magazines. Do you want clients reading articles about the latest investigation into a rogue financial company?
- Financial trade magazines. Do you want clients reading "How to Sell More Life Insurance to Your Clients"?
- Advertising literature. They already made it to your office. Now is the time to focus on dreams, not products.
- Strange-looking pictures on the walls.
- Old furniture.
- Decor that doesn't look like it was put together well.

The lobby should contain:

- Magazines on travel, golf, architecture, living on the coast, and the like. You want people to start dreaming when they sit down in your office.
- Nice, comfortable furniture.
- Classy pictures and art.
- Decor that's well done, cohesive, and aesthetically pleasing.

Your office should not:

- Have papers and client files stacked up and spread all over the desk/tables/floor.
- Have graphs of the stock market hanging on your wall. Why get people worried about the volatility of the stock market as they step into your office?
- Seem highly disorganized and messy.

Your office should contain:

- Lots of family pictures.
- Awards and accolades you've received.
- Artwork/pictures that relax people—water scenes, travel scenes, and so on.
- Decor that is well done and classy.

MEDIA ACTION POINTS

- ✔ Make your lobby a decompression zone.
- ✔ Consider hiring a decorator to help you, or enlist the help of someone whose style you appreciate.
- ✔ Create an office that is an oasis for clients where they relax and buy from you.

CHALLENGE

As you appear more frequently in the media, you'll begin to develop your unique reputation and image. You'll create and solidify a personal brand that people will begin to recognize, accept, and ultimately turn to for sound financial advice. It's important to understand what your prospective clients expect in a financial professional and then work daily to exceed those expectations. As a hardworking financial professional, your reputation is on the line with each new client you work with. As you consistently provide quality financial advice and service to your clients, they will reward you with a steady stream of referrals and new business. When you combine your client service with how well you come across in the media, you will place yourself on the path to becoming a recognized financial expert in your local area. And you'll become identified by your unique and respected brand of financial planning. In the next chapter you'll discover how you can take your unique brand and use it to make more money for you and your business.

CHAPTER SIX

GETTING THE BUSINESS

N ow that you've learned how to break into the media and become the financial expert in your local area, it's time for you to leverage your newfound media exposure into tangible sales for your business and more money for you. It all comes down to the bottom line. This is why you've been interrupting your schedule to answer reporters' questions. This is why you've been getting up early to be interviewed at your local television or radio station. The primary goal of your media exposure is to increase your visibility, credibility, and profitability.

The more your ideal prospects see you or your name in the media, the more likely they'll be to call on you when they need your services. In this chapter you'll learn the "insider" secrets of using the media to make you money. These are the strategies you can implement to help transition your successful media involvement from a simple marketing tool to an effective means of increasing your sales and creating the business you've always dreamed about.

Now that the prospective clients—who are calling you after seeing your media appearances—feel like they already know you, it's absolutely critical for you to connect the knowledgeable media personality they have come to know with the financial professional with whom they expect to work. It's important to remember that they have begun to form opinions about you from your media exposure. They may think of you as knowledgeable. Or they may consider you trustworthy. They may view you as a very caring person. Their opinion of you is what leads to their expectations of you—how they expect you to run your business and work with clients.

EXCEEDING THEIR EXPECTATIONS

Here are some common expectations people have of financial professionals who appear in the media or who are in the public eye:

- *They are very busy.* When people call you after seeing you in the media, they often begin by saying, "I know you're very busy. We (watch you, listen to you, read about you) all the time. Would you have time to meet with us?"
- *They don't work with everyone.* When people see you as the expert in the media, they may assume that you're a specialist, not a generalist. Often they will ask, "I know you don't work with everyone, but would you consider working with us? We only have a couple hundred thousand to invest. I don't know if that's enough for you to do anything with."
- *They have a nicely decorated, professional office staffed with friendly, knowledgeable people.* When people see you in the media, they view you as successful. When they come to your office, you want them to feel pampered and impressed. The first impression coordinator (your receptionist) should "wow" them. And your office decor should make it apparent that you work with high-net-worth clients and have an appreciation for the finer things.

Simply put, it's critical to meet or exceed potential clients' expectations when they first speak with you and when they arrive at your office. People form opinions quickly after meeting someone for the first time. Stack the deck in your favor by creating an office environment that communicates the message that you're successful. Table 6.1 presents three phases to securing business from people who initiate contact with you based on your media appearances.

Table 6.1   Three Phases of Client Relationships

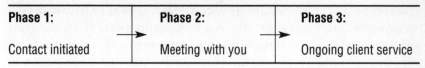

Phase 1:	Phase 2:	Phase 3:
Contact initiated	Meeting with you	Ongoing client service

PHASE 1: CONTACT INITIATED

Phase 1 is the "contact," whether direct or indirect, you have with your prospects before they actually come in for an appointment. It includes all the media work you've been doing so far—from the first time a prospect sees you on television or your name in the newspaper, to the day that prospect decides to call or e-mail you. Your media appearances have been laying the groundwork and increasing both your visibility and your credibility in the eyes of your ideal prospects. But it's not until those prospects begin calling you that you can turn your media work into increased profitability for you and your practice. The steps you take after setting the appointment can help solidify your reputation in the eyes of your prospects and can help nudge them closer to becoming your clients.

When you set an appointment with a prospect, the first thing you should do is to mail the prospect written materials that describe you and your services in detail. Those materials should include what I call a bio (biography) letter. The purpose of the bio letter is to establish your credibility firmly before prospective clients walk into your office. Then, when they meet with you, they are free to enjoy their surroundings and get to know you better, without any lingering doubts about whether you are smart or qualified enough to help them with their financial matters. As you begin appearing in media venues, be sure to list your various media appearances in your bio letter. To get the biggest bang from this letter, it needs to be sent from someone else, such as a branch manager, your partner, or your office manager. If the letter comes from you, it may come across that you're bragging, and you don't want to create that impression. Done correctly, this letter will let prospective clients know that you have the credentials and experience to be their financial professional of choice. When prospects meet with you for the first time, they sometimes say that they enjoyed reading your resume. At such times, it's best to play dumb as to how the letter was sent. It's best to say something like "Did they send that out again? Well, I guess it's no secret that I love what I do—helping clients reach their financial goals." This statement allows you to come across as someone they'd like to work with, but it also makes you look humble.

Sample Bio Letter

Date

Contact Name
Address
City, State Zip

Dear (Name):

We're pleased that you've decided to explore your options for achieving your financial goals through (insert company name). (Insert your name) is a well-regarded advisor and will be personally following up with you. Here is his brief personal biography:

BACKGROUND

- Appears weekly as Channel 4's Financial Expert
- Has appeared nationally on Bloomberg Television as a Financial Expert
- Quoted on CBS Marketwatch.com as a Financial Expert
- Financial column published weekly in *The Chicago Business Press*
- Quoted as a Financial Expert in *The Chicago Times*, *The Illinois Reader*, and CBS Marketwatch.com
- Named a member of the exclusive ABC Financial Top Advisors group
- Specializes in working with clients who are a few years from retirement or already retired

LICENSES

- Chartered Financial Consultant
- National Association of Security Dealers (NASD) Series 7 Securities Dealer's license

- Illinois Securities Dealer's license
- Illinois Life and Health and Disability license
- Certified Financial Planner

EDUCATION

- BA, Finance, University of Chicago

COMMUNITY INVOLVEMENT

- Board of Directors, Rotary Club of Chicago
- Named "Rotarian of the Year"

(Your first name) is one of the most recognized (financial advisors/stockbrokers/ financial professionals/accountants) in the local area. You will find that he exhibits the highest ethical standards and sincerely cares about the goals and dreams of his clients. (Your first name)'s diverse experience also gives him a unique insight into the financial planning challenges facing those that are close to retirement or already retired.

Sincerely,
(Name of other person with signature)
(Title)

The second part of this phase is to establish a professional appointment confirmation process that your staff implements. Typically this process includes three steps:

1. *When the appointment is set,* your staff should mail out a welcome letter, a map to your office, the "bio" letter, and a help sheet. (See samples that follow.)
2. *A week before the appointment,* your staff should mail a reminder postcard.
3. *The day before the appointment,* your staff should call and remind the prospect and confirm the appointment.

Sample Welcome Letter

Date

Contact Name
Address
City, State Zip

Dear (Name):

Thank you for your time the other day. I look forward to meeting with you on (insert meeting date and time). Please find enclosed a map to my office.

This initial consultation is an exploratory visit which will give you an opportunity to find out about (your company name) and how we work with people to help them more effectively reach their financial goals. It will also give me an opportunity to learn more about you and your own individual financial goals. There is no charge for this initial visit. And, of course, everything we discuss is strictly confidential.

You may want to give some thought to your goals and assemble any documents that you feel would be helpful for me to understand your present situation. To make this easier for you, I have enclosed a help sheet for you to fill out.

I look forward to meeting you.

Sincerely,

(Your Name), (any Professional Designation letters)
(Title or Professional Designation)

Enclosures: Map, Help Sheet

Sample Help Sheet

Help Sheet

To help you get started on financial planning, we have included this Help Sheet. Use it, and you'll have a much better idea of where you stand today. Yet it's tomorrow that really counts. Your financial advisor can help you develop a personalized plan that will help you meet your particular needs and goals.

Figuring Your Net Worth

Property Assets

Residence	$_____
Vacation Home	$_____
Furnishings	$_____
Jewelry & Art	$_____
Automobiles	$_____
Other Property Assets	$_____

Fixed Assets

Government Bonds	$_____
Municipal Bonds	$_____
Corporate Bonds	$_____
Face Amount Certificates	$_____
Fixed Dollar Annuities	$_____
Other Fixed Assets	$_____

Equity Assets

Real Estate	$_____
Stocks	$_____
Mutual Funds	$_____
Variable Annuities	$_____
Business Interests	$_____
Other Equity Assets	$_____

Liabilities

Home Mortgage	$_____
Other Mortgage	$_____
Bank Loans	$_____
Auto Loans	$_____
Personal Loans	$_____
Charge Accounts	$_____
Other Debts	$_____
Total Liabilities	**$_____**

Cash Reserve Assets

Checking Accounts	$_____
Savings Accounts	$_____
Credit Unions	$_____
Certificates of Deposit	$_____
Other Cash Reserves	$_____
Total Assets	**$_____**

Family Net Worth

Total Assets	$_____
Total Liabilities	$_____

(Subtract your liabilities from your assets)

Net Worth	**$_____**

Figuring Your Net Cash Flow

Monthly Income

Wages, Salary (after taxes) $_____

Dividends from Stocks, Mutual Funds, etc. $_____

Interest on Savings Accounts, CD's, Bonds, etc. $_____

Capital Gains $_____

Other Pensions, Royalties, etc. $_____

Total Monthly Income $_____

Monthly Discretionary Expenses

Cable TV $_____

Dining $_____

Dues $_____

Entertainment $_____

Gifts to Charities $_____

Gifts to Family & Others $_____

Hobbies $_____

Recreation $_____

Subscriptions $_____

Travel $_____

Other (pets, allowances, kids' sports, etc.) $_____

Monthly Committed Expenses
Housing

Mortgage Payments $_____

Rent $_____

Home/Rent Insurance Premium $_____

Real Estate Taxes $_____

Utilities $_____

Other (lawn, snow, etc.) $_____

Food, Clothing, Transportation

Food/Groceries $_____

Clothing $_____

Auto Insurance Premium(s) $_____

Auto Loan Payments $_____

Auto Maintenance (oil, fuel, filters) $_____

Vehicle Tax $_____

Other (tolls, bus, taxi) $_____

Other Committed Expenses

Alimony	$_____
Bank Charges	$_____
Charge Account/Credit Card Payments	$_____
Child Support	$_____
Dependent Care	$_____
Education Costs	$_____
Home Improvements/Repairs	$_____
Loan Payments (other)	$_____
Medical Costs	$_____
Other Deductible	$_____
Other Pre-tax	$_____
Prescriptions/Drugs	$_____
Personal Care (hair care/dry cleaning, etc.)	$_____
Premiums (disability insurance)	$_____
Premiums (life insurance)	$_____
Premiums (long-term care insurance)	$_____
Premiums (medical insurance)	$_____
Premiums (umbrella insurance)	$_____
Premiums (other)	$_____
Telephone (local, long distance, cellular)	$_____
Unreimbursed Employee Expenses	$_____
Total Monthly Expenses	**$_____**

Net Cash Flow

Total Monthly Income	$_____
Total Monthly Expenses	$_____

(Subtract your expenses from your income)

Discretionary Monthly Income   **$_____**

Note: Income and expenses often vary greatly from month to month, especially if you receive bonuses, have high winter utility bills, or pay your taxes at certain times. You may therefore wish to plot your cash flow through all 12 months or take a 12-month average.

These documents set the tone, prior to the meeting, that you run a very professional business and are highly organized. You're letting prospective clients know that your time is valuable and you don't want to set an appointment that will be missed or canceled. People who are serious about their money—the type of clients you want to have—typically find this approach reassuring. They want to feel that the person helping them manage their financial affairs runs her business in an organized manner, because it gives them confidence to know that their money will be handled capably.

Let's examine this appointment confirmation process from a client psychology angle. Many people view financial professionals as nothing more than salespeople. Because of that, it can be very difficult to win these people over and secure them as clients after just one visit with you. You have to implement a battle plan that will change prospects' perception of you from that of a salesperson to that of a trusted, knowledgeable financial professional. Because prospects have most likely seen you in the media or read your quotes in various newspaper or magazine articles, you are already in their minds. The bio letter outlining your background and abilities, which they receive after setting an appointment with you, reinforces their idea of you as a professional, as do the appointment letter, the help sheet, and the appointment reminder call. They expect to receive this information from medical professionals; receiving it from you reinforces prospects' notion of you as the financial professional they want to work with.

MEDIA ACTION POINTS

Here's a recap of what to send out before your first appointment:

✔ A bio letter about you from someone else or a professionally printed bio card with your picture

✔ A letter of introduction, with the date and time of the appointment listed and a description of what they should expect in the meeting and what they should bring

✔ A financial help sheet—a one- to two-page listing of their assets, liabilities, income, and expenses

✔ A map to your office (if appropriate)

PHASE 2: THE FIRST APPOINTMENT

This is your opportunity really to stand out to your prospective clients. Affluent investors like to be treated with a high level of respect and want to feel that they are receiving special attention. They want to know that the financial professional they have selected is monitoring their situation, keeping them updated on potential changes that may need to be made or possible investment opportunities. Perhaps most important, ideal clients want to know that their financial advisor cares about them as individuals, instead of feeling that they are "just another client." How do you convey this in your initial meeting? First of all, it is important to review the seven-step process prospective clients have come through so far:

1. Prospective clients see you in some form of the media and view you as a financial expert. Most likely they have been following you for a while, and a "triggering financial event" in their lives has prompted them to contact you.

2. Prospective clients call in. You either speak to the person then or you call back to introduce yourself personally and set up an appointment. Prospective clients are impressed that a "busy financial expert" had time to visit briefly with them.

3. Your office mails prospective clients the bio letter (from a ranking person at your office) or a bio brochure, and they read about how you work with clients, what your education/credentials are, your interests and your family, and they see your picture again. Prospective clients appreciate getting to read more about you personally.

4. Your office sends prospective clients an appointment reminder and makes a confirmation call. This allows the prospective client to begin to build rapport with your office staff.

5. A member of your staff warmly greets prospective clients when they arrive at your office and offers them a beverage. As the prospective clients sit in the lobby to wait for their appointment, they don't see magazines about the stock market and world politics, which would make them anxious and preoccupied. Instead, they can select from magazines that illus-

trate the world's most beautiful vacation destinations and most elegantly decorated homes. This helps them relax, and they begin to daydream about one day affording the kind of luxuries described in the magazines.

6. You come out to meet the prospective clients. Your big smile, direct eye contact, and firm handshake makes them feel at ease as you lead them to your office.

7. Prospective clients enter your personal office and look around, pleased to see prominent pictures of your family and a nicely decorated office. Research has shown that one of the top desires of affluent clients is to spend more time with their children and grandchildren; thus they are delighted to see that you also place high importance on your family. They also gaze for a few moments at the artwork above your conference table—and comment that it reminds them of a trip they took recently.

To be candid, most of the "selling" of yourself has occurred before you even sit down in your office with prospective clients. This is one of the things that sets apart top-notch financial professionals, who their clients view as consultants, from those advisors whom clients view as salespeople. What a huge difference it makes to have prospective clients presold on you before you even begin your presentation! This way you spend almost your entire time together getting to know them as people—their goals, their fears, their dreams. This is the beauty of appearing in the media on a regular basis.

Now picture the opposite scenario—the one many advisors find themselves in right now. Instead of prospective clients coming to their office ready and willing to do business, they arrive feeling defensive and prepared to be sold something. These advisors spend most of the meeting establishing their own credibility with prospective clients and making a case as to why they should work together. Because such advisors have to spend so much time tooting their own horns to get the prospects to accept them as qualified professionals, they have little if any time to spend truly getting to know clients. Obviously, these financial professionals have not been in the media and do not have the firm foundation of credibility laid before the prospective clients came to their offices. But *you* will, if you've followed the steps laid out in this book.

One of the best ways to stand out to ideal clients is to come across as a true professional. After all, they've gotten to know your "style" through the media, and they like that style. If they didn't, they wouldn't be in your office today. So now it's time to leverage your prospective clients' perception of you by creating an environment where ideal prospects become excited to do business with you.

First let's identify the characteristics of an ideal client:

- Very receptive to receiving advice
- Meets your minimum investment preference:
  - Can invest X amount of money ($100,000, $250,000, $500,000, $1,000,000)
  - Has a large insurance need (life, disability, long-term care, health, etc.)
  - Has significant monthly discretionary money to invest
- Is not happy with his or her present situation or financial professional
- Already wants to work with you before he or she has even met you

Let's now review the 7-step process that I use as a financial professional with my prospective clients. I want to invite you into my office as I meet with an ideal prospective client. This approach has worked consistently for me and the countless other advisors that have implemented it.

STEP 1: HAVE AN AGENDA

If you talked to the prospective clients on the phone, did you find out their financial concerns and why they want to meet with you? If you suspect that they have sizable assets and fit the criteria you're looking for in new clients, type up a quick agenda for the meeting, listing the key points of what they told you on the phone. When clients sit down in your office and you give them each a copy of the agenda, which is customized and lists some of their specific concerns, they realize immediately that you pay attention to details. By providing this agenda, you've already begun to solidify your relationship as their new financial professional.

Sample Agenda that I Use with My Clients:

Meeting Agenda
CONFIDENTIAL

Date: (insert date)
For: (insert client name)

1. Notes from initial conversation:
   Ages:
   Goals:
   Children:
   Concerns:
   Investments:

2. What questions do you have for me?

3. Review your financial situation

4. Discuss your financial goals and concerns

5. Review how I work with clients

6. Schedule next meeting

STEP 2: GET TO KNOW THEM BY ASKING KEY QUESTIONS

Think about when you go to see the doctor. The doctor typically asks you a lot of questions: "Does it hurt here?" "How does that feel?" "How long have you had this problem?" Doctors have mastered the open-ended question approach. You want to approach your client meetings in the exact same way. When prospective clients step into your office, you become the "financial doctor" diagnosing their financial ailments. By asking lots of open-ended questions, you allow people to open up to you about their financial goals and dreams. Once you've gained their trust, they'll rely on you to recommend the appropriate financial products that will benefit them the most. If you connect with people on an emotional level first, they will be more likely to work with you because you kept your priorities straight when you met with them: the relationship with them first, and their money second.

I have found these to be 12 powerful questions to ask potential clients:

1. How long have you been married? (This question allows them to reminisce.)
2. Do you have children? (Write down names and ages and where they live.)
3. Do you have grandchildren? (Write down names and ages and where they live.)
4. Does your family get along with each other? (This question will catch them by surprise. It gives you insight into how they run their family.)
5. What type of work do you do? (for those still working)
6. What type of work did you retire from? (for those retired)
7. Walk me through a typical day at your job. (for those still working)
8. Walk me through a typical day for you. (for those retired)
9. What do you like to do for fun?
10. What are the most important things to you right now?
11. What are your financial goals?
12. What would be the greatest service I could provide for you?

Each of these questions will help open up your relationship with prospective clients. Try to delve deeply with each question. The deeper you go, the more quickly you will make a connection that may cause them to work with you. These questions make you stand out as a consultative financial professional, not a salesperson trying desperately to make a sale.

Most of us dislike the "selling" process. When we walk into an environment where it's likely someone will try to sell us something, we begin throwing up defense mechanisms. We immediately view the situation negatively. As a consultative financial professional, you want to remove this fear by asking questions and demonstrating your interest in your prospective clients. By positioning yourself as the trusted financial expert, you will not only put people at ease, but you also will create a desire in them to work with you, because you come across as a true professional.

MEDIA ACTION POINTS

✔ Use an agenda in your meetings.

✔ Ask insightful questions that cause your prospective clients to really think.

✔ Remove the fear from your prospective clients' minds by positioning yourself as a true financial consultant, not a salesperson.

STEP 3: REVIEW THEIR FINANCIAL SITUATION

Now that you've gotten your potential clients to open up and give you some insight into them as individuals, you have established the critical foundation of rapport. Your next step is to review their financial situation. You say, "Let's go ahead and review your financial situation. Do you have the Help Sheet we sent to you?"

At this point, prospects generally reach into their file and present the sheet to you completely filled out. Why does this happen frequently? Because prior to their arrival in your office, you and your staff subtly established the expectation that those who want to work with you as their financial professional must be serious and have their ducks in a row. Now you simply go through the Help Sheet while taking notes about the items listed. If they didn't complete the Help Sheet, begin writing down a list of their current investments, assets, and liabilities. As you review each investment they have, ask a few questions to better understand them as investors. Ask these four investment insight questions:

1. How did you pick this particular investment?
2. How has it done for you?

3. Is this something you'd like me to review to see what other options are available to you? (With this question, you're setting the stage for prospective clients either to transfer that particular investment to you or exchange it for something you feel is more appropriate for their situation. This also gives them the opportunity to tell you that they want you to manage this particular investment.)

4. Do you have any investments or insurance policies that are off limits to me? In other words, even if I could find a way to help save you money on your insurance or identify some investment options that may be more suitable for you, is there anything you wouldn't want to change? (This question helps you know exactly what dollars the client will be moving to you and clearly identifies the other items that you have no possibility of managing.)

As you review their current financial situation and begin reviewing their existing investments, insurance policies, debt situation, and discretionary income, you'll be able to determine whether the prospects you're meeting with fit your ideal client profile and whether you want to take them on as clients.

Let's stop here and evaluate your next steps from a client psychology standpoint. By this point, you've engaged the prospective clients and you've gotten them to open up about their financial goals, dreams, and families. Your credibility has been confirmed by the way you've listened, what you've said, and how you've conducted the meeting so far.

Think of your meetings with prospects like a marathon race, as illustrated in Table 6.2.

By the time your meeting is drawing to a close, your prospective clients are thinking about several things:

- I wonder if I have enough money for this financial professional to work with me?
- Can I afford to work with this person?
- This is exactly what I've been looking for.
- How do we get started?

Table 6.2   Four Stages of a Successful Appointment

Running a Race	Prospective Client Meeting
1. Warm-up/loosening up	1. Greet your guests with a warm smile and reassuring handshake.
2. Start fast	2. Quickly begin to get to know them by asking lots of questions and listening intently. "Test-close" throughout your presentation by asking, "How do you feel about that?" and "Is this the approach you're looking for?"
3. Stay focused on the race	3. Confirm in your mind that these are the types of people you want to work with. Analyze how "advisor-receptive" they are and determine whether you can provide them value and if they will be profitable for you.
4. Finish strong	4. Begin your closing with the mind-set of a highly successful professional who is about to convert a prospect into a client.

It is also common for people to tense up a little when they are about to be "sold" something. Knowing this fact about human nature, you want to do everything you can to be perceived as the consummate professional. You have built up your credibility and relationship with prospective clients throughout your time together. At the end of the meeting, you don't want to appear that you're trying to pressure them into working with you or that you have to make a sale today. Remember, if the meeting has gone well, it's very likely these prospects are ready to work with you. In their minds, the purpose of this meeting was to confirm that you truly are the person they thought you were.

Table 6.3 shows what to do as you close your meeting with prospective clients and give them the "call to action."

If you feel the prospective clients are a fit, move on to Step 4 below. If you feel they are not a fit (perhaps they don't have your preferred level of assets, have too much credit card debt,

Table 6.3 Purpose-Driven Meeting Wrap-Up

Your Action	Their Reaction
• Move your chair back, sit back, and look relaxed.	• "He's relaxed so we'll be relaxed."
• Put your pen down.	• "He just wants to talk with us."
• Speak slowly and in a lower tone of voice.	• "He is conveying a thoughtful and serious tone."
• Restate their goals from memory.	• "He was listening and really understands what we're looking for."
• Use open gestures (no crossing of your arms, speak with palms up, etc.)	• "He's not rigid or tense. He's being up front and honest with us."

can't save enough money each month, etc.), then here is what you can say:

> Now that I've had a chance to find out your goals and review your financial situation, let me describe the way I work with clients. I work with clients (insert your description—examples: on a fee basis, by charging them a yearly fee, with X level of investment assets, who can typically save at least X dollars per month, etc.). My primary goal is to provide value to you. Let me give you two options: First, you can work with me at a cost of X dollars per year. Here's what that would include: meeting two to three times per year, monitoring your investments, doing a financial plan, and being accessible throughout the year. The other option would be for me to refer you to another financial professional on my team. Her focus is to help clients like yourself, and her business is structured to work with clients who may not be able to pay a yearly fee. Which option would you prefer?

If they choose to go with you, they've now committed to paying you a yearly fee, so you will get paid for your time and you're not taking on clients who are less than desirable. If they choose to work with another financial professional to whom you refer them, you can receive a split of the business as a referral fee from that advisor.

It's a win-win situation: Potential clients win by getting to make the decision, and both options lead them to take action to improve their financial situation. You win by getting paid for your time, no matter which option they select. However, if your inner voice is telling you not to work with someone, listen to it. More often than not, it is a warning sign letting you know that avoiding these clients now can spare you problems down the road.

MEDIA ACTION POINTS

✔ Carefully review your prospective clients' financial situation.

✔ Use the Help Sheet.

✔ Determine whether they are a fit for you as clients. If not, offer them two options: working with you for a set fee or working with another advisor.

✔ Only take on clients whom you have a good feeling about.

STEP 4: DESCRIBE YOUR SERVICES (HOW YOU WORK WITH IDEAL CLIENTS)

Once you have an understanding of prospective clients' financial goals, and you've identified that they are, indeed, the type of clients you'd like to have, it's time for you to describe how you can help them. Say something like this:

> Now that I understand what your goals are and I know where you stand today financially, let me describe to you how I work with clients. At the beginning of our meeting, you said you were concerned about (list their goals and concerns that you wrote down in your notes; for the best effect, say them from memory, looking directly at the prospective clients). That's exactly the type of work I do for my clients. Here are some ways I could help you (list some of the services you provide). Is that what you'd like my help with?

(If they answer "yes," continue talking. If they answer "no," stop immediately and have them clarify what it is they want you to do for them. Once you've identified that, then continue.)

> I specialize in working with clients (describe your target market, so they know you are a specialist, not a generalist—for example: "who are a few years from retirement or are already retired. My expertise is in helping people transition from earning a paycheck to having their investments generate a paycheck for them each month."). Does that make sense? I need to tell you that there is no shortage of financial professionals that you can work with. Let me first describe what I'm not. I'm not going to do a financial plan for you, invest all your money, and then never contact you again. If that's the approach you want, I am not the advisor for you. I also will not call you each week with a hot stock tip. If that's what you're looking for, then I am not the advisor for you.
>
> What sets me apart from other financial people is that I am a specialist. The work we do for our clients is all custom-tailored just for you. Your plan will be different from every other client we work with because everyone we work with is different. Clients who work with us want a long-term relationship. What you're paying me to do is provide you with your investment options.
>
> Here's the way I work with clients. You are not hiring me to tell you what to do with your money. My role is to provide you with options that will help improve your financial situation. All of the investment options that I present to you will be good, but I want you to select the option that you're most comfortable with. I'll go over the good and the bad points of each of the options and then let you decide which ones you'd like to choose. You may say, "Well, we want you to tell us which option you recommend." And I'll be happy to do that. But my point is that we'll work together as a team. You have accumulated the level of dollars you have now without my help and I respect that. So if we think of yourselves as the owners of (insert their last name) Corporation, then think of me as your chief financial consultant. Does that approach make sense? Is that what you're looking for?

Again, wait for a response. If they don't agree clearly, stop and begin asking questions to determine what they want. Once they've clearly specified what they are looking for or you have answered their questions, continue.

> Here's how I work. I am primarily a (insert words like "fee-based advisor," "fee-only advisor," "comprehensive financial advisor," etc.), so my clients pay me a yearly fee to provide financial guidance to them throughout the year. That fee is based on the complexity of your situation and the time it will take me and my staff to provide the appropriate level of advice and service to you. The yearly fee in your situation would be approximately $X per year. As part of that fee, we will put together a detailed financial analysis that shows where you stand today. Then we'll design a game plan that is custom-tailored for you and your goals, which will show you each of your investment options. Then I'll help you implement your financial plan. We'll have the paperwork ready for you to move accounts, open new accounts, and so on. Then I will begin to monitor your accounts throughout the year. We also will meet (quarterly, twice per year, etc.). I like to meet with you frequently because, with the size of your portfolio, it's important to monitor it on a regular basis. I will also call you and e-mail you throughout the year to keep in touch. Now, I need you to know that I am not perfect. Ask my (husband/wife), and (he/she) will verify that. I can't predict the market. My crystal ball broke a long time ago. Since I am not perfect, I can try to communicate perfectly with you. I think of your money like my money. We want to do all we can to help you achieve your financial goals. Is this the type of service you're looking for?

If they answer "yes," proceed to Step 5. If they answer "no" or indicate anything that is not a clear "yes," begin asking more questions to determine what type of service they are seeking. Then proceed to Step 5.

MEDIA ACTION POINTS

✔ Describe your services.

✔ Describe whom you work with (your ideal clients).

✔ Describe how you are paid.

✔ Stop frequently and ask if what you're describing is what they are looking for in an advisor.

STEP 5: THE HIGH-NET-WORTH FINALE

What I'm about to illustrate for you flies in the face of how most companies train their financial professionals to "close" their prospective clients. In my experience, I have found that lower-tier prospects respond to traditional closing techniques of asking for the check right now. The ideal prospects you want don't respond well to this old-line approach and require a completely different tactic. Let's be honest: If you have a million dollars to invest, will you decide in just one day who will handle that money? Of course not. Don't fool yourself into thinking that prospective clients will want to be pressured into making a quick decision. Instead, use one of the following options to end your meetings.

Option 1:   Meet Next Week
Say:

> Let's schedule another time to get back together. I'd like us to meet again next week to keep the momentum going that we've begun today. How does that work with your schedule?

If they say "yes," continue. If they say "no" or begin asking other questions, stop and answer their questions before continuing.

After you've agreed on your next meeting date and time, say:

> I want you to go home and consider what we've talked about today. Here's what I'd like you to think about: I want you to really get a picture of what you want to do in retirement (or whatever their main financial goal is). How much monthly income would you like, what kind of trips do you want to take, and what do you want to accomplish in retirement? We covered a lot of ground today, but we're really going to delve deeply into your retirement goals in our next meeting.
>
> Now, on your way home, you'll probably realize that you forgot to ask me something. So what I'd like you to do is write down any questions you have and bring them with you next week. Here's our agenda for our meeting next week: First, I'll answer any questions you might have. Then we'll go back over your financial goals. Then we'll focus on your retirement. Next we'll discuss the pros and cons of the investment and insurance options available to you. I'll spend the majority of the meeting asking a lot more questions so I completely understand your situation. Then

at the end of the meeting, we'll fill out the financial planning paperwork to get things started. How does that sound to you?

I think we covered a lot of things today, and I feel that it was very productive time. How do you feel about we talked about today?

Discuss any questions or concerns they might have, then close with "Great! I'm looking forward to seeing you next week."

Option 2:   Get Started Now
Go through the conversation in option 1. If prospective clients are giving you clear indications that they want to get started today, give them the option of filling out the paperwork then or waiting until they come back next week with a scheduled appointment. If they're ready to go, get out the paperwork for them to become new clients.

However, if you misread them and they surprise you by saying "Oh, no, we need to think about this," you can say, "Of course. I wanted to give you the option of either getting started today or waiting until we get back together." Keep in mind that asking them to become clients during your first meeting is a risky proposition. After all, you've been working to create a perception of yourself as a consultant and a specialist. Being perceived as pushing for the business today can put a serious dent in your credibility armor.

Remember, the goal of this close is to make you stand apart from any other professional. People naturally expect you to try to "close" them on the deal. Handling it in the opposite way from what they expect will solidify in their minds that you work with affluent people all the time. After using this approach for many years and seeing it work consistently, I can tell you that it's well worth the additional week it adds to your selling cycle. Remember to use your instincts to know when to use option 1 or option 2.

MEDIA ACTION POINTS

- ✔ Don't pressure ideal prospects to become clients during the initial meeting unless they clearly tell you they want to get started now.

- ✔ Use the nontraditional sales approach and give your prospects one week to clearly define their goals before signing the paperwork in their next meeting with you.

Step 6: Meeting Follow-up

On the same day that you meet with the prospects, hand-write a thank-you note to them:

> (Their names),
>
> I enjoyed our time together today. I felt that it was a very productive time and we covered a lot of information. As we discussed, please think carefully about your retirement goals and what you would like to do and accomplish in retirement. I'm looking forward to helping you achieve your short- and long-term financial goals. See you next week!
>
> Sincerely,
>
> (Your signature)

Insert your business card and mail to them. Few people hand-write thank-you notes anymore. By writing one, you'll stand out in people's minds. Encouraging people to take a week to solidify their decision to work with you and following up your meeting with a handwritten thank-you note sends a clear message that you are a top-notch financial professional who truly understands the needs and concerns of people with sizable amounts of money.

MEDIA ACTION POINT

✔ Handwrite a thank-you note after the initial meeting, mentioning the goals you talked about with the prospects.

PHASE 3: ONGOING CLIENT SERVICE

One of the key principles I have learned from being part of my local Rotary Club is this: Those who serve best, profit most. Service can mean how you serve your clients, employees, family, or community. Profit can come in the form of money, having a family that loves you, or having a network of meaningful friendships. As sales guru Zig Ziglar says, "If you help enough people get what they want, you will then achieve what you want." By putting the needs of others above your own, you place yourself in a position to reap the benefits from the seeds of helpfulness you've sown. Plus, when people see you helping others, they are even more happy for you when you are successful.

I have found that people with money like to feel special and that they are part of their financial professional's select group of clients.

Here are some simple steps you or a member of your staff can implement as part of your Client Service program to help your clients feel special.

- Jot a short note on a copy of your top clients' statements each month saying: "(Client name), I was just reviewing your accounts. Let's continue the current plan.—(your name)." Your note is short and sweet, but it lets your clients know that you're watching things.

- Send a monthly newsletter by e-mail or regular mail. If your company makes client-approved market commentary available, then use that.

- Call your clients when you think about them. You may be driving to the office or working on another task when a client pops into your head. Call them right then and say, "I was just thinking about you and wanted to give you a call." Often, clients will say to you that they were just about to call you about something. By being proactive, you can pleasantly surprise clients and quickly answer a question or handle an issue that came up.

- Send birthday cards to your top clients.

- Send Christmas cards to your top clients. Include a family picture. This is a great way to show off your spouse and/or children to your clients. Remember, research shows that family is one of the most important concerns of affluent clients.

- Establish a meeting routine with your clients. (Have your staff call and confirm the appointments.) Consider quarterly meetings for top clients and meetings every six months for the rest of your clients. This routine helps ensure that you are on top of things in your clients' lives. Research shows that if more than six months go by and clients haven't met with their financial professional, they begin to feel that they aren't important anymore.

The key question to ask yourself is this: What can you do to provide service to your clients and help insulate your book of business from the competition? Remember, your clients are being actively solicited to move their money to another advisor, even as you read this. Always be thinking of new strategies to show your clients that you care about them and they are valuable to you. It's a lot less expensive to keep an existing client than it is to find a new one. By implementing what I have described, you'll have happy clients who will refer other similar clients to you. Plus, you'll enjoy your business a lot more because you'll experience less negativity from your clients.

MEDIA ACTION POINTS

✔ Serve your clients.

✔ Always think of new ways to show your clients how much they mean to you.

✔ Insulate your client relationships by meeting and communicating with them regularly.

LEVERAGE THE MEDIA TO ALLOW PROSPECTIVE CLIENTS TO REACH YOU

At the end of the day, the goal of all the work you do in the media is to increase your visibility, credibility, and profitability. It's one thing to begin appearing in the media, it's another thing altogether to use the media effectively to bring in business. It does take time to begin creating a name for yourself in the media. But the quicker you implement these direct business-building strategies, the sooner you will establish a streamlined system to allow prospective clients to reach you easily. First you must focus on appearing in multiple media outlets on a frequent basis. Then you must concentrate on maximizing those appearances.

Here are some examples of ways to maximize your media appearances in each media outlet.

Newspaper/Magazine/Internet

Interview. If a reporter calls you to be one of the people he will quote in his story, be sure to give him the correct spelling of your name, your title, and your company name. For example: "Joe Smith, an Investment Specialist with ABC Financial Company . . ."

Guest Article. If you have the opportunity to write a guest article for a newspaper, include in your tagline at the bottom of the article a couple of ways for people to contact you. For example: "Joe Smith is an Investment Specialist with ABC Financial Company and specializes in working with clients who are near retirement or already retired. He can be reached by phone at (222) 555-1234 or by e-mail at jsmith@abcfinancial.com."

Important note: Remember that newspapers, magazines, and Internet news sites typically don't call the people they interview financial experts. Provide the media with your company title. For example: Financial Advisor, Investment Specialist, Vice President of Investments.

Television

Interview. If you are contacted to be interviewed on TV, the producer will ask you how you want your name and company name to appear on the screen as you're being interviewed. For example: "Joe Smith, ABC Financial." When they interview you, have them refer to you as a "financial expert."

Program Listing. Many TV news stations list their upcoming guests for the week on their web site. If your station can do this, ask them to list your name, company name, title, and where your office is located. For example: "Financial Expert Joe Smith of ABC Financial Company in Chicago gives our viewers tips on how to save enough for retirement."

Station's Web Site. If you become a regular guest on a news program, have your contact information included on the station's web site. It's also good to include a direct link that readers can click to send you an e-mail question or be transferred to your own web site. For example: "Dollars & Sense with Channel 4 Financial Expert Joe Smith. Joe Smith is an Investment Specialist with ABC Financial Company, with offices in Chicago. Joe specializes in working with clients who (briefly describe common ideal client concerns)." Include your picture, a brief personal biography that mentions your spouse and children (if applicable), your hobbies, your address, phone and fax numbers and e-mail address, and that you are currently accepting new clients. Check with your compliance department to get approval on this and include any other information it requires such as a listing of the states you're licensed in.

Anchor Endorsement. The more you are interviewed, the more you'll get to know the news anchors who are interviewing you. As they grow more comfortable with you, they may comment during or after the interview (while still on the air) about how knowledgeable you are. For example, as you are ending an interview that went well, the anchor may say, "Joe, you're always a wealth of information for our viewers," or "Susan, thanks for giving us some great information today!" These subtle media endorsements are very powerful in letting the viewers know that you are that station's "financial expert" and that even the news anchors appreciate your advice. As I've discussed, always treat the news anchors like royalty. They can have a big impact on the success or failure of your media efforts.

Radio

Story Interview. If a radio station reporter calls you to ask a question about a news story, often your comments will be edited down to a five-second sound byte that will be played during the newscast. So that you can be identified properly on the air, the reporter will confirm how you want your name read, your company name, and where you're located. Tell them to refer to you as a financial expert.

Live Interview. If a radio station producer calls you to do a live interview, it may be by phone or in person. For an interview by phone, you call in to the station and the anchor or reporter asks you questions about a specific topic. Typically, this is for a 5- to 10-minute interview. An in-studio interview typically is longer and may involve a combination of answering questions from the anchor and answering live call-in questions from listeners. In both instances, the anchor will refer to you as, for example: "Financial Expert Joe Smith with ABC Financial Company in Chicago." Ask for your phone number and/or e-mail address to be read on the air so listeners can contact you with their questions. Tell listeners that the next time you appear on that station, you will answer their questions on the air.

Station's Web Site. If you become a regular guest on a news program, have your contact information included on the station's Web site. List the same information given for a television station's Web site.

The bottom line is that it's not enough simply to appear in the media. That's only the first step. The second step is to be identified clearly as a financial expert by the media and to receive their implied endorsement. The third and most profitable step is to establish contact points through each of your media appearances for prospective clients to reach you easily and set appointments.

MAXIMIZING YOUR CELEBRITY STATUS

How will you know if your work in the media is being noticed by others? People will begin to walk up to you and tell you that they saw your name in the paper or they enjoyed watching the interview you did on the local news. You will begin to stand out in their eyes. Their assumption is that because you are the one the media is calling on to provide financial insight, you must be the expert. People who are in the media automatically receive a certain level of respect. When you become classified as a media personality, your standing automatically will be elevated in the minds of your prospective clients.

Here are some strategies to leverage your media exposure through the organizations to which you belong:

- Give back to the community in some way. People respect and admire those who do. Their opinion of you will skyrocket when they see someone they recognize as a local celebrity giving back to the community. The more you appear in the media and the more active you are in your community, the more your reputation will grow as a professional who is both generous with his time and very knowledgeable about finances.

- Select one or two organizations or social causes to be actively involved in. Joining more than two sometimes does more harm than good, because you won't be able to be active and highly visible or to make a big impact on the organization(s).

- Take a position of leadership within the organizations you choose. That way you're in the know and can play a vital role in the decision-making processes, thereby demonstrating your leadership skills.

- Allow the organizations you're a part of to leverage you, the media personality. An organization's board members can lend it tremendous credibility. If you're a recognized and respected financial expert in your local area and you're on the board, that makes the organization look good. Volunteer to speak to different groups on behalf of your organization, and be introduced as "the financial expert as seen in (name the media outlets)."

As I discussed earlier, when people see you being quoted frequently in the newspaper, they view you as a financial professional who really knows his stuff. When they see a picture of you giving an award at your local school to deserving students, they view you as a person who really cares about the community and the future of the next generation. When they meet you in person, they view you as a caring, knowledgeable financial professional who is well rounded. When all those pieces come together, your prospects will begin to view you as *their* financial expert.

Just because you appear in the media once doesn't mean your phone will begin ringing off the hook. Appearing frequently will establish your credibility in the minds of prospective clients, credibility that may cause them to work with you. One of the biggest benefits of appearing in the media as a financial expert is that you have an advantage on your competition. Remember, there is no shortage of other financial professionals vying for your existing clients' money and trying to reach the prospective clients you want. But when people see you in the media, they will begin to wonder why *their* financial professionals aren't in the media.

MEDIA ACTION POINTS

✔ Get involved in one to two organizations whose causes you really believe in.

✔ Become recognized as a leader in the organization so that you're highly visible.

EXTENSION MARKETING

Once you've begun appearing in the media, immediately begin to work on extension marketing, where you can parlay your media exposure into other client marketing opportunities, such as seminars, where people who already feel they know you can meet you in person and shake your hand. Because the attendees feel they already have a relationship with you, you can focus on answering their questions and building rapport instead of worrying about touting your credibility, which you've already established through the media. Appearing in the media can create tremendous exposure and excellent opportunities. By learning how to capitalize on that exposure, you'll have the potential to start making the big money. Through hosting seminars, you can leverage your media exposure and translate that into more clients and more profit for your practice. When people connect the media personality to your reassuring smile and confident handshake, your media campaign comes together and the money begins to flow.

LEVERAGE THE MEDIA FOR SEMINARS/EVENTS

Seminars are one of the best ways to market in the financial services industry. Many of my clients tell me that they receive several invitations each month to attend dinner seminars. I have conditioned my clients to keep me updated on what marketing solicitations they receive. The financial professionals mailing these unsolicited invitations haven't built name recognition or a relationship with those people receiving the mailing. People receiving these invitations are likely to accept only if they're eager for a free meal at a fancy restaurant.

Because many financial professionals don't see this reality, they become frustrated that they've fed a lot of people without gaining any new, ideal clients. After all, those who do show up at such events have their defense mechanisms set in high gear, afraid of being sold something. These poor financial professionals have to spend a significant part of the program just establishing their credibility. That's valuable time they could be spending extolling the virtues of services or products.

There's a better way, and here it is: When you appear in the media, you are a recognized financial expert. If you're consistently following my suggestions on how to speak to the media, you're positioning yourself as both highly intelligent and down-to-earth. Now it's time to move from people simply watching you or listening to you, to providing a way for them to meet you—the viewer or listener seminar. Here's how it works: Once every few months, you organize the (media outlet name) Viewer or Listener Seminar. The process can be broken down into five steps:

1. Select a catchy financial topic.
2. Find a nice restaurant to cater the event.
3. Contact your financial wholesalers to help pay for the event.
4. Approach the station about putting up a graphic while you're speaking (if on TV) or have the announcer (if on radio) tell about your upcoming seminar. (I have had the best success with announcing this seminar for 10 to 14 days leading up to the event.)
5. Ask one of the anchors to attend the seminar as your special guest.

This can be a huge benefit the station offers to its viewers/listeners as a way for them to meet their financial expert in person and be treated to a special evening.

If you follow these steps, you'll provide three compelling reasons for people to attend:

1. To meet you in person and hear you discuss a financial topic of interest to them.
2. To have a nice meal free of charge.
3. To meet the news anchor who is your special guest in person.

Many people consider the news anchors they watch or listen to as their trusted friends. Therefore, the opportunity to meet an anchor in person is a nice treat for them. It also provides you with an implied endorsement from the anchor. Unlike traditional dinner seminars, where people have never heard of the financial professional conducting the event, they know you and you've already established a high level of credibility in their minds. So you can spend the entire evening focusing on people's key concerns and offer them just enough strategies and ideas to capture their interest, so that they'll take the next step of meeting with you and then working with you.

Let's say that you approach your media outlet about promoting your seminar and it says "no" to the idea or says that you have to buy advertising time. First of all, it's generally best not to pay for any advertising on your station. Here's why: Once that station realizes that you have the ability to pay, it will begin to look at you differently. Then, the moment you stop paying for advertising, it is very likely that you'll be dropped from the station altogether. Let me caution you: Don't mix your free media appearances with paid advertising. It's a combustible combination that often blows up in a financial professional's face. If the media outlet does say "no" to your idea of a Viewer/Listener Seminar, then consider another alternative of promoting the seminar all on your own. But what will set your seminar apart from all the other solicitations that prospective clients receive is that you will be identified in your material as the (media outlet name) financial expert. You could write something like: "You're cordially invited to Joe Smith's Retirement Success Seminar. You've seen him on Channel 4. Now is your opportunity to meet him in person, enjoy a great meal and learn about your investment options for retirement. RSVP today to . . ." Even though your media outlet didn't let you promote the seminar on the air, you still can invite one of the anchors to be your special guest.

This type of seminar significantly speeds up the selling process for prospects, who are quicker to implement your investment and insurance recommendations. Think about this seminar from a buyer psychology standpoint. The people who show up feel like they already know you to some degree. Essentially, they are spending the evening looking for a reason *not* to work with you. Your primary goal at each seminar is to make sure people like you. Assuming you get to shake hands and have some "face time" with each person who attends, and your presentation really addresses their concerns and fears and offers potential solutions, it is highly likely they will check the box on your seminar evaluation sheet that says "I'm interested in a meeting."

MEDIA ACTION POINTS

✔ Plan and implement a Viewer or Listener Financial Seminar.

✔ Choose a catchy financial topic that will appeal to your ideal prospects.

✔ Find a nice restaurant to hold the event.

✔ Contact the wholesalers you work with and ask them to help pay for the event.

✔ Approach the station about promoting the event. Have viewers or listeners call your office to RSVP.

✔ Ask one of the anchors or program hosts to attend.

✔ Make sure you have a chance to speak personally with all who attend.

VIEWER OR LISTENER E-MAILS AND QUESTIONS

As you work with the media and the opportunity arises for you to be a regular guest on a particular program, you will begin to attract a loyal following. The first step is for you to have your e-mail address and phone number published on the station's web site so people can contact you. One way to sell this idea to your media outlet is to say that you want to answer viewer or listener questions on the air. People love to have their questions answered, and it is a great way to showcase your vast knowledge of a wide range of financial issues. Call-in shows, where you answer viewer or listener questions, are very popular. Whether you are taking questions live on the air or you have the questions in advance and simply answer them on the air, people will be interested.

It's important to answer questions that you feel will have a wide appeal to your audience. When people hear a question being asked, they often think about how it applies to their own situation. The best way to respond to viewer or listener questions is to give general advice and suggestions, since you don't have knowledge about a person's entire financial situation. For example, you could mention an idea that has worked for other clients, but then qualify it by saying you don't know whether it would work well for their particular situation. This is also a way to get the audience to take the next step of calling you or setting up a time to visit with you. Add people who e-mail questions to you to an e-mail prospecting list, which you can use to send out a periodic e-newsletter. Over time, you can accumulate a large number of e-mail addresses of prospective clients whom you can invite to seminars or other client events.

MEDIA ACTION POINTS

✔ Talk to your producer about setting up a regular segment where you answer viewer or listener questions.

✔ Choose questions that address topics that will interest many people.

✔ Offer general advice and suggestions, not specific recommendations.

SPEAKING TO ORGANIZATIONS

Public speaking is one of the best ways to help you connect your "media financial expert" personality to that of an approachable and

friendly financial professional. People have an unquenchable thirst
for timely and relevant financial information. When the expert that
they see or hear in the media on a regular basis speaks to them in
person on important financial issues, they are very likely to sit up
and take notice. Published lists of all the organizations in your local
area can be great sources of leads to schedule public speaking opportunities. Another great opportunity for public speaking is simply
to let the media outlets you work with know you would be happy to
speak on their behalf. Many event planners for local organizations
call the media outlets to ask their anchors and popular guests to
speak at their events. When you speak at these events, you carry the
implied endorsement of the media outlet, which is very powerful.
At such events, it's best to spend time talking about your family, the
organization you're speaking to, and the challenges you've helped
clients overcome. Also discuss the general trends in the stock market and provide some financial ideas that will peak the interest of
those in the audience, so they'll be interested in contacting you for
more information. But *never* make any type of sales solicitation from
the podium. People don't want to feel that they're being sold anything, especially at a charitable function or event.

MEDIA ACTION POINTS

✔ Let organizations know that you are available to speak to them.

✔ Obtain a list of local organizations and start contacting them.

✔ Let your TV/radio stations know that you are interested in speak-
    ing to any organizations that may contact them.

✔ When you speak to an organization, do not attempt to solicit
    business during your presentation.

ALWAYS A NEW AUDIENCE

In many ways, your local area is like a revolving door. Every day new
people move into your local buying area. Some get transferred
from their existing companies, some take new jobs, and some may

be retiring to be closer to their grandchildren. At the same time, other people are moving out of your area for the exact same reasons. This constant flux of residents presents a clear marketing opportunity for you. There are always new, qualified prospective clients moving into your area who have no idea of who you are. That means that you always must be marketing yourself through the media as a financial expert. Seek out as many media opportunities as you can, because with each interview you'll be targeting a different audience of prospective clients. Many people in your local audience are very interested in moving their investment and insurance accounts to a local financial professional like you. It's all a game of getting to them first and being the financial expert who comes to their minds.

Picture this scenario: New residents flip on their television and see you as the financial expert. Then they see your name in the business section of the newspaper, where you're quoted. Then they get a letter from you with your professional bio, which you mail to new residents in your area. All this exposure means that you are greatly increasing the likelihood that these people will call you when they need help with their financial planning. Of course, the reality is that these move-ins will get solicited from many financial professionals. But since your media exposure is already cementing your reputation as the local financial expert, the marketing you direct toward these people will stand out. Why? Because everyone wants to work with an expert, not a salesperson. That's the power of the media!

As you speak in the media, consider occasionally speaking on topics that are of particular interest to new residents, such as:

- The benefits of transferring investment and insurance accounts to a local advisor
- Your state's laws in regard to financial account ownership and beneficiary designations
- Your state's estate planning laws

The key is to *never stop marketing yourself*. The moment you stop, someone else may take advantage of an opportunity that should have been yours. You must change your entire business philosophy and realize that your business is a mega-marketing company that just happens to provide sound financial planning.

MEDIA ACTION POINTS

✔ New potential clients are always relocating.

✔ Always be marketing yourself so that new residents choose to work with you.

USE THE MEDIA FOR PROFITABLE PROFESSIONAL ALLIANCES

One strategy often pitched to financial professionals is to establish relationships with certified public accountants (CPAs) and attorneys as referral sources. Research has shown that clients place a high level of trust in these professionals. If a CPA or attorney recommends you to clients, those clients will typically be very receptive to you as their financial professional. Although these can be excellent initiatives to pursue, establishing effective professional alliances can be time-consuming, and they often lead to little, if any, business coming your way. How can you make these relationships work?

It's important to look at this from the viewpoint of CPAs and attorneys. They are regularly solicited by many other financial professionals, just like you, wanting to set up a reciprocal business relationship with mutual referrals. Because they are approached so often, most CPAs and attorneys can't possibly refer clients to all the financial professionals they know. As a result, advisors often feel frustrated and begin to view this as a one-way relationship benefitting only the CPA and/or attorney. Thus, they drop this marketing opportunity too soon.

Remember that professional relationships take time to pay big dividends back to you. To stand out from the pack of other financial professionals vying for these opportunities with CPAs and attorneys, you have to be creative in your approach. You need to position yourself as the ideal choice for a trusted and knowledgeable financial professional, so other professionals can feel comfortable and confident referring investment and insurance business to you.

Here are five proven strategies to capture the attention of CPAs and attorneys:

1. Approach CPAs/attorneys as the (media outlet's name) financial expert. Let them know that because of the media work you do, you have clients asking you to recommend qualified CPAs and attorneys to them. Find out if they are taking on new clients and what types of ideal clients they are looking for.

2. Approach CPAs/attorneys as the (media outlet's name) financial expert. Let them know that in your media work, occasionally your media outlet needs to interview a CPA or attorney. Ask if you can refer the media to this person. Generally CPAs and attorneys will be flattered and say yes.

3. Contact CPAs/attorneys and let them know that you are a safe and trustworthy choice to refer clients to for investment or insurance help. Assure the professionals that you will speak highly of them and work to protect their existing relationships with the clients. Let them know that once their referral becomes your client, you will never refer that client's tax or legal business elsewhere. CPAs and attorneys like to know that their business will be protected from competitors trying to steal their clients.

4. Tell CPAs/attorneys that part of your procedure is to run your investment and insurance recommendations by them first before showing them to the clients they have referred to you. This way, the CPAs or attorneys are kept in the loop and feel that they are still in control. Most CPAs and attorneys sincerely care for the welfare of their clients and want to make sure that they receive only the best advice. When you review your recommendations with the CPAs/attorneys first, they will have a chance to see how you work with clients. They'll also feel confident and trust in your abilities to help them provide sound financial planning for their clients.

5. Approach CPAs/attorneys with the idea that you are beginning to market yourself aggressively in your local area to bring in ideal clients, and you're looking for CPAs/attorneys who are also looking to attract ideal clients and grow their practices. Doing this can lead to your giving seminars to-

gether and other joint marketing initiatives that can help forge long-term, mutually profitable relationships.

Often CPAs and attorneys view financial professionals as nothing more than commission-based salespeople. The deck is stacked against you from the beginning. By being tenacious and by working diligently to build long-term relationships with these professionals, both you and the professionals you work with can profit. It takes a lot of patience on your part to forge a successful professional alliance relationship. Leverage your position as the media's financial expert. Consistently working on the relationship may result in long-term business-building opportunities.

MEDIA ACTION POINTS

✔ Build professional relationships with at least one CPA and one attorney, so that each of you can refer business to the others.

✔ When you approach these professionals, think about what you can do to help them get what they want.

✔ Always keep the CPA/attorney "in the loop" on what you're recommending to their referrals.

BE THE "GO-TO" PERSON

People are attracted to people who can help them solve their problems. For this reason, it's important for you to position yourself as a "connector" of people. If your clients have a need, make sure that you know a trustworthy person you can send them to who can solve their problem. As your reputation grows from your media exposure and from the good work you're doing for your clients, those clients will begin to think of you as a person who "knows everybody." For example, clients may need you to recommend CPAs or attorneys that specialize in a certain area to help them with a tax or legal issue. Continually add to your list of reputable people you can refer people to when they need assistance that you can't provide yourself. The larger your list of "key references" is, the more professionals are out there referring their clients to you as well.

STAY IN COMPLIANCE

Finally, as you continue your media initiatives, it's important to work closely with your firm's compliance and communications departments and be aware of their rules and regulations. Most firms won't have a problem with your media appearances as long as you're getting across the company's message and values and not making outlandish promises. Often you can stay in compliance merely by sending the compliance department videotapes of all TV appearances, cassette tapes of all radio interviews, and copies of newspapers or magazines in which you were quoted. In some cases, prior approvals may be necessary for guest articles. Remember, the compliance department is there to help.

As you appear in your local media, let your firm's national media relations department know. That way, if a national media opportunity comes up and it needs an experienced advisor to do the interview skillfully, it can call on you.

CONCLUSION

You now know the secrets to capturing the attention of the media and proactively creating interview opportunities. By implementing what you've read in this book, you'll soon be attracting the clients you've always wanted, making more money, and living the balanced life of your dreams. To reap the media's rewards of visibility, credibility, and higher profitability, you'll have to work hard. But believe me, it's worth it. Remember back to Chapter One when Mary finally made the call to the financial professional whom she discovered in the media. As you read this, countless people like Mary are looking for a trusted and knowledgeable financial professional, but they don't know whom to select. Consistently follow the program I have outlined and you'll be putting yourself in a position to be a recognized financial expert in your local community and the first choice of your ideal prospective clients. Now is the time for you to be the one media outlets call on. You have the tools; Simply use them. Success is yours for the taking. Go for it!

30 Days to Creating a Marketing Mentality

Read this statement aloud every day for 30 days so it becomes a habit and a new way of positive business thinking for you.

Today I choose to take control of how I market myself. It is my daily responsibility to seek out new and exciting opportunities to create massive exposure for me and my business. I am confident and knowledgeable, and there is no better financial professional for ideal clients to work with than me. The only limitations I face are the ones I imagine in my own mind. Today I will be brave and courageous and step outside of the comfort zone that has held me captive for too long. Today I choose to be successful and accomplish great things.

INDEX

Take the next step on the path to becoming the financial expert you were meant to be!

You've just discovered the master strategies to attracting your most ideal and profitable clients through the media. Now continue to implement your new-found knowledge to make getting into your local media even easier and more profitable! In this 9-step how-to packed program, Derrick Kinney expands the strategies and insights he shared in *Master the Media: A Personal Marketing System for Financial Professionals* and takes them to a whole new level, with a CD-ROM program that gives you all the tools and templates you need to get started right away. Simply use the power of your computer and begin to experience media success.

Derrick Kinney's Popular CD Program, INSIDER MARKETING SECRETS *REVEALED!* is packed with *even more tips, techniques, secrets, strategies, and bottom-line insights you won't find anywhere else.*

The CD-ROM includes:

- A 10-day Quick Start Plan to get you in the media right away.

- An easy system for getting the names of your local media contacts.

- The proven fax and e-mail press release templates to get you results fast. Simply add your information and send—it's that simple!